Aspects of
Spirituality and Education

Aspects of
Spirituality and Education

Chief Editor
R.P. Sharma

Editor
Arti Srivastava

Kaveri Books
New Delhi-110 002

First Published in 2013
ISBN 978-81-7479-123-8

Published by
Kaveri Books
4832/24, Ansari Road
New Delhi - 110 002 (India)
Tel.: 011-2328 8140, 2324 5799
Fax: 011-2328 8140
E-mail: kaveribooks@vsnl.com,
kaveribooks@gmail.com
Website: www.kaveribooks.com

Laser Typesetting by : Deep Graphics, Delhi

PRINTED IN INDIA

FOREWORD

Every epoch creates its own ethos, its focal point , its defining metaphor, encapsulating its needs, drives, aspirations and its civilizational pursuits. Going by what meets the eye, the present generation appears to be riding the currents and cross currents that replenish our basic biological and some psychological needs, at times delimiting the time honoured 'intellectual pursuits' which do register their presence, more as escapades than as living-credos. However the discerning mind does record the sub-terraneous sounds and fury, suggesting the turmoil that engulfs the learning millions. While half the population of the world is engaged in its grim struggle for managing its basic needs, others are seeking solace in pleasures and pursuits that oppulance can procure. Only a microscopic minority of the so called 'intellectual' class, justify its existence by venting venom on the established system of different variants. The gross has eclipsed the inner enlightenment of the man, masquerading energy even though momentarily.

But then the silver lining encircling dark clouds promises that all the gloom is only a passing phase. The human spirit is inherently equipped to come out triumphant in all those trials and tribulations. There are enough signposts, in the form of value vectors left by scriptures, saints, sages and servants of the past and the present who could steer humanity to its spiritual destiny, its *Eldorado.*

However spirituality, the ultimate goal of our existence, is wrapped in mystery. The multiplicity of the whole concept should have opened up varied pathways to achieve its realization. Instead, it has allowed different denominations and religious institutions to underscore their own endeavors, while a few pushing their own strindent dogmas and blinding prejudices not withstanding. However our ancient *Rishies* and other liberated souls have, from a universalistic pedestal, proclaimed that the ultimate reality is one even though there are many ways to reach *it. (Ekam* Sad *Viprah Bahudha Vadanti).* The inquisitive and the aspirants have sought and achieved fulfillment through the chanting of the sacred verses(Mantras), and hymns articulating sound (*NadaBrahma*). Others followed the 'Book', the printed word, as the mandate from heaven, still others drew their strength and security from a prescribed code of conduct. There have been highly enlightened souls, *Swami Vivekananda, Sri Aurobindo* to mention a few, who committed their lives to the suffering humanity (*Janata Janardana*) Meditation of different genres offers its own effectivity for those who delve deep into the inner self. There is no dirth of some awakened minds who hold science as an appropriate scaffolding for upholding their convictions in this field. All these spiritual route- maps have their own legitimacy.

This book is a bold attempt to decipher its multivocal connotations. The whole idea has emanated from a Seminar on the theme organized by the *Army Institute of Education, Delhi Cantt,* through the efforts of *Dr. Neerja Dhankar,* Principal of the Institute and other colleagues and administration. The anthology is a symposium of various facets of this sublime subject creditably edited by Dr. Arti Srivastava and assisted by some other friends of the faculty. Apart from highlighting different dimensions of this abstract theme widely known as Spiritual Quotient in educational parlance, the authors represent different disciplines and dispositions—some offering their lived experiences, others deconstructing the concept from their heart while others exploring the spiritual space through intellect, all committed to *Loka Sanghrah*–the good of the people. If the readers get even a fine and a short glimpse of Rodin's *"Thinking Man'* and the *Kamakura (Buddha's statue)* of Japan, the two ends of the spectrum encased in the book, this humble presentation would have realized its objective "OM *SHANTI SHANTI"*.

R. P. Sharma

CONTENTS

INTRODUCTION

A. Nature of Spirituality

Intimations of Spirituality: The author Prof R P. Sharma has traced "the evolution of the spiritual Odessey of Man" From the times when man was led to propitiate the heavenly bodies; 'conceptualized an anthropomorphic God before arriving at the conception of the ultimate reality as 'qualified' and then 'unqualified' Brahaman. Traversing through the Weltanshaung of the Indian philosophical tradition he takes the reader from the Vedic period to its resurgence in the contemporary thought of Sri Aurobindo. He leads the pilgrim to arrive at the "realization that one is heir to the noblest inheritance of immoratality."

In, '**Our Self–in the light of Thich Hanh's Understanding**': the author Dr. Neelam Mehta Bali holds spiritualism as a belief in the Perfection of Life and looks forward to exploring and being peace as a process integral to understanding self and working towards realization of that Perfection.

'**Spiritual Unity in the thought of Sri Aurobindo**'. Exploring this title the author Dr. Arbind Kumar Jha asserts that spirituality is the very basis of all education. The essence of his chapter in his words is, "the humankind now has a collective responsibility to facilitate the construction of a shared global culture through spiritually oriented educational socialization." .... Within this context it is critical that we reflectively contemplate what we teach and how we teach. He presents a plethora of gems from Sri Aurobindo's understanding of Man, his vision of the process of Man's evolution in the larger context of Life Divine

Advaita Vedanta of Sankara: The author Dr.Reena Kannojiya begins with the premise that education utilizes all the forms of philosophy - wisdom, ideas and critical inquiry in developing particular point of view which in turn helps in developing a thought or tradition. In ancient times education was imparted to those who were curious to know about the phenomena of this world and beyond this world. In this chapter Dr.Kannojiya gives an exposition of the conceptual wealth of Advaita Vedanta of Sankara and analyses it as being matter of education. It is because 'Advaita Vedanta theory of consciousness provides a solution to the analysis of epistemological and metaphysical issues involved in the problem of Self. The author has also explored the ethical aspects of Sankara's thought that conceives value as phenomenal reality i.e. dharma and nominal reality i.e. Brahman. Brahman can be realized by pursuit of knowledge, devotion to GOD and purity of Atman.

YOGA : The Eternal Panacea. "True to the spirit of the title of the paper the author Ms. Savita Sharma begins with a reference to a number of scriptures and their Understanding of Yoga from different perspectives. To begin with she quotes Patanjali's definition of Yoga as 'Chitta -Vritti-Nirodha' and then proceeds to dwell on deliberations of Swami Krishnanandaji of Life Divine Society and Swami Shivanandji to finally state that all expositions of Yoga emphasise the disciplining of the mind to achieve the Grand Union. She reiterates that the truth of our self and its relation with the Universe are but inseparable aspects of the same reality. Herein the role of mind is underlined. This is followed by deliberation on the nature of mind and its functions as well as its source or origin. She concludes that

Universal consciousness expresses itself through Cosmic Mind or Hiranyagarbha. Discussing Universal consciousness as Existence, Sharma takes cognizance of the duality in our way of life. The mind on one hand creates an understanding of the phenomenal world, while on the other hand mind itself is the creation of the Absolute. Hence minds urge to strive for Perfection or to be complete, and hence the compulsion to act. Actions and reactions form a continuous chain. Mind is caught in the predicament of action and non-action. Actions which bring one closer to Perfection let the mind rest in the Absolute. Mind is released from tyranny of death and desire. A process of conscious evolution-arriving at YOGA. Existence is Co-extensive with all knowledge and knowledge is consciousness. The author concludes that the Tao of YOGA is to "change the attitude and direction of Mind from individuality to universality."

B. Spirituality-the educational pathway.

This section discusses the role of education in the realization of Spirituality.

In '**Spiritual development through education-Swami Vivekananda**' Dr. Panneerselvam thinks that Vivekananda's perspective can be a solutions of all social and global evils through education. He feels the dire need of awakening man and his spiritual self wherein, he thinks, lies the very purpose of education. The aim of education is to manifest in our lives the perfection, which is the very nature of our inner self. This perfection is the realization of the infinite power which resides in everything and every where–existence, consciousness and bliss. After understanding the essential nature of this perfection, we should identify it with our inner self. For achieving this, one will have to eliminate one's ego, ignorance and all other false identification, which stand in the way. Meditation, fortified by moral purity and passion for truth helps man to leave behind the body, the senses, the ego and all other non-self elements, which are perishable. Education, in Vivekananda's understanding enables one to comprehend one's self within as the self everywhere. Man making for Swamiji stands for rousing man to the awareness of his true self. However, education thus signified does not point towards the development of the soul in isolation from body and mind.

In '**Realizing Self through Aesthetic Experience**', Dr. Arti Srivastava has talked about the role of aesthetics for the realization of Self. She feels that aesthetics in the form of appreciation and creation helps individual to relate himself with the world outside and then to relate to himself through the process of expression. This relationship can be understood as an aesthetic dialogue where the artist and the creation interact and develop sensitivity for each other which help them to discover their creative self. The chapter is influenced by Tagore's philosophy of Ananda Yoga.

Prof Joneja in '**Education for Spiritual Development in School students**'. believes that spirituality is traditionally thought in relation to religion or equated with religion and not beyond it. She has talked about Spiritual Intelligence (SI) or Spiritual Quotient (SQ) with which persons address and solve problems of meaning and other higher values of life. She feels that the schools engaged in seriously educating students for the Fundamental Duties of Citizens contribute to students' spiritual development. She has mentioned her NCERT experiences and believes that the teachers without formally naming it, in other words unconsciously, are contributing to spiritual development of students by their own conduct, example, during teaching-learning activities related to subject matter or other school experiences.

In '**Story Telling for Spiritual Education**' Dr. Pranita Gopal has shared her experiences related to the students of preservice teacher education program. She used story telling as a pedagogy for Spiritual Education. She invited stories from the learners and allowed reflection to sensitize learners spiritually. 'The idea worked successfully with the author. She has mentioned a few stories also in the chapter.

Spiritual Education according to her begins from the realm of knowing the surroundings and transcends into the dimensions of knowing thy self and in process knowing about the process of knowing and ultimately takes an individual to the realm of the limitless.

Dr. Aradhana Mani in '**Fostering Spiritual Development through Education**' has talked about Spiritual development as the development of a sense of identity, self-worth, personal insight, meaning and purpose. She emphasizes the development of a pupil's 'spirit', 'soul', 'personality' or 'character'. Independent approach, integrated approach and subtle approach are the three approaches which are being emphasized by Dr. Mani to impart value based spiritual education. She feels that the need of the hour is to educate the student community on the significance of spirituality in their life and for that the educators themselves must be role models.

In '**Spiritual Development-need of the hour**' Dr.Manisha Manocha presents the viewpoint that the main concerns of spiritual development are metaphysical, value and religious practices and symbols. She has talked about the reflective aspect of spiritual development and relates it to human existence. She feels that spiritual development contributes towards the development of certain qualities which will make the world a place of peaceful co–existence. The child should be assisted in his personal search for identity and the understanding of the world.

C. Values, Education and Spirituality

This section signifies a relationship between values, education and spirituality.

'Value of Education vis-a-vis Value Education-Swami Vivekananda's Fundamental Thoughts on Education and their Practical Application in the Present day Context. In this chapter Swami Atmapriyananda, has discussed Swami Vivekananda's fundamental thoughts on education and their practical application in the present-day context. He thinks that due to the explosion of enormous and mind-boggling variety of information, the one main concern of the human brain is to store and retrieve information. Man has invented super giant computers to become a support for the purpose. Modern education is only working to fulfill this desire of man and thus becoming insensitive for higher emotions, richer perceptions and deeper sense of values. Value education according to him is very important to connect man with the higher Self which is the very source of all values. What Swami Vivekananda predicted more than hundred years ago appears to be fast becoming realizable. Swami Vivekananda's fundamental thoughts on education and their practical application in the present-day context thus assumes an increasing relevance for the resuscitation of the basic human values in education.

'Toward A New Era of Value Creation' by 'Dr. Diasaku Ikeda'.– Dr. Sadhana Srivastava has adapted the writing of Dr. Daisaku Ikeda who has talked about the aim of creating peace and harmony in the society. She feels that we are living in an era marked by an absence of values, in which no measure of worth other than the monetary is recognized. We need to develop the awareness that the standard of values that judges human worth solely on the basis of economic capacity, represent the effective absence of values. There is a growing concern that new humanitarian crises may arise in different part of the world unless targeted assistance addressing the needs of these populations is provided. Three concrete areas where measures should be taken concern employment, children, and the empowerment of women.

Dr. Neerja Dhankar in **'Spirituality in Action 24 x 7'** thinks that ultimate and highest aim of education is developing spirituality. She feels that present day education is preparing students for better economic pursuits only and not for healthy physical, mental, social and spiritual life. Spirituality is part of daily life according to her and she strongly feels that through very simple routine it should be made into our habits.

Expanding Spiritual Space

This section connects to spirituality through different approaches.

Prof. Gauri Srivastava in her chapter on "**Thoughts of Eminent Indian Thinkers**",has made an attempt in her paper to highlight the thoughts of some eminent men and women of India on education of girls and women. It talks about reflection of the inner spirituality of women of India. Spirituality according to her is when one has the innate courage to speak, voice opinion without fear and any kind of intimidation. She has mentioned the writings of eminent thinkers and the way they have linked social, economic and political progress of India with the improvement in the status of women. She feels that by changing the existing social structure and by interpreting sacred text we can understand the status of women. Women according to her enjoyed a relatively better position in Vedic period She has mentioned various methods which were advocated by the reformers in bringing about a change in the existing social institutions In the context of education, she finds that education would make women rational, aware and improves the overall quality of their own life, and also of women folk in successive generations. Further, educated women would themselves spearhead social, educational and political reforms that would help in creating a voice of the voiceless and help in generating women's perspective in all development activities.

In the chapter "**Mahatma Gandhi and Bhagvad Gita**", the author Dr. Y.P. Anand gracefully enriches the thought and thinking of the reader by citing innumerable reflections of Mahatma Gandhi on Gita. **Gandhi** had faith in Gita, and over a period of time his mentor Raychandbhai made him realize the necessity of diving deeper into it ... it became his infallible guide of conduct ... a ready solution of all-troubles and trials. Words representing virtues ..e.g. aparigraha [non-possesssion] and samabhava..gripped him. Gandhi reflected "GITA is the living, life giving, immortal Mother." In his highly informative paper Dr. Anand reveals that Gandhi has given most comprehensive, contemporary and even revolutionary meanings and interpretations of Gita. 'Gandhi has written more works on Gita than any other Bhashyakar,' is another one of the eye opening statements of the author. He concludes his article by citing select extracts from Gandhi's, "Introduction to - GITA as Anasaktiyoga."

Dr. Amita Puri in her article '**Integrating spirituality and psychotherapy**', talks about the importance of integrating spirituality in everyday living, which shapes the way we think, perceive, act and respond. She maintains that the psychopathology of today's world can be assuaged and mitigated if we have a firm perspective of spirituality. Scientists in the present day world, globally opine that, man has a better chance for achieving happiness provided he integrates spirituality in his very being, reflected in his day to day activities.

Section-A

NATURE OF SPIRITUALITY

CHAPTER–1

INTIMATIONS OF SPIRITUALITY

— Prof. R. P. Sharma

There is a need within the soul of man,
The splendours of the surface never sate,
For life and mind and then glory and debate,
Are the slow prelude of vast theme,
A sketch confused of a supernal plan,
A preface in the epic of the supreme

- Sri Aurobindo (collected poems - Page-137)

And I have felt
A presence that disturbs me with the joy
Of elevated thoughts; a sense sublime
Of something far more deeply interfused
Whose dwelling is the light of the setting suns
And the round ocean and the living air,
And the blue sky, and in the mind of man:
A motion and a spirit that impels
All thinking things,all objects of all
And rolls through all things.

-William Wordsworth
Lines composed a few miles above Tintern Abbey]

I had uploaded my mind with these two thoughtscapes before I could ever construe the meaning much less the essence, of the two extracts quoted above It would be rather audacious to say even now whether I have fully absorbed the 'blessed mood' of the two visionaries one dwelling in the supramental plane and the other thoroughly immersed in panentheism. However there is a growing realisation that this theme lifts one out of the quagmire of the world that environs me, you and others representing the modern times.

I presuppose that the trials and tribulations of the present times are so engaging that we are left with no respite to ever concentrate on what makes us a special species, the crown of God's creation. The problems of humanity at large and the bounty of nature around, do not enter our mental radar, until these directly impact our personal existence. In our pursuit of facticity of things we have gone to the extent of objectifying our own person.

Any sensible mind could conveniently monitor the mood of the modern times induced predominantly by sheer negativity. God is conspicuous only by his absence–wherin denominational sects, proxying Godliness fail to provide relief.

People find palliatives in only rave parties, in junk food, in jazzy sound and funky colours. The jacked up enjoyments in so called getaways only turnout to be occasional episodes in a melodramatic theme that valiantly tries to put life on even keel. The margins of the illusive Elysium keep on receding as one staggers towards them. In fact the ill defined ends digitalised are approached through the vehicles that are driven by technical rationality. All the blessings of the technological age fail to provide copula, the connecting lever that could integrate the fragmentary world around us into a meaningful, purposeful existence. All this happens because our means do not match our ends.

Some thoughtful and sensitive poetic minds paint this age of anxiety, inhabited by the culturally uprooted and spiritually displaced, in stark dismal colours. Sample these lines in this context–

.............crazed we come and coarsened we go
our wobbling way: there is a white silence
of antiseptics and instruments.
At both ends, but a babble between
And a shame surely.

-W.H.Auden: Age of Anxiety
[Cited in Jugal Kishore Mukherjee's Man Human to Man Divine p.183]

But this enchantment experienced by a modern man is an over reaction in response to the transient aspects of our present day humdrum existence. It is so because in the fast paced life of today, the contigent has upstaged the perennial. The sparkle without has bedimmed the spark within. The satiation of the 'senses' has devalued the search for the 'essence of life'.

This phase in the history of mankind is lamentable, however the darkness that envelops today is not lasting. There is light at the end of the tunnel, as there have been attempts, quite variegated, on the part of Man to reach it. And this grand narrative of typically human endeavour has not yet seen the end of the day.

In tracing the evolution of the spiritual odyssey, we find that loaded by two powerful urges of self preservation and the curiosity to know the power that presides over natural phenomena and the tenure of his existence, man was led to propitiate the heavenly bodies i.e. the Sun, the Moon to mention a few. In this epochal essay ancient Indians were arguably in the vanguard in establishing a living relationship with the cosmos. The next stage in the pilgrimage was to *know* the first cause of the universe which awakened them to conceptualise Godhead as the sovereign governer of the Cosmos. The fertility of the human ingenuity made it possible to envisage an 'all pervading super- intending power' or an anthropomorphic God, who regulates the universe. The history of various civilizations is a monumental proof of this all encompassing search.

The Indian visionaries equipped with intuition and articulated wisdom, arrived at the conception of the ultimate reality as 'qualified' and then 'unqualified' *Brahman.* The Vedanta of the Advait genre markcd this culmination of human quest for the final and efficient cause of the Universe. They had graduated from the prevedic pastoral culture to a philosophical one, as expressed in the *Upanishads,* the *jnanakanda* of the Vedas.

Some other civilizations have come up with their own efforts and theocratic theorizations notwithstanding. That the wisdom of their impact, *upanishads* has left the highest watermark in spiritual stirrings', unmatched sublimity and profundity, is not just a sentimental outburst of an Indian believer but comprises the sanest voices recorded in world history. The spiritual march of man had traversed the cosmological era, then tenanted the theological sojourn and had enlivened the most abstract theorisation of beautitude, the end of this phase of spiritual journey.

However the discerning minds, equipped with that Promethein spirit have telescoped the destinations that, lie ahead of *Brahman,* the Atman. R.D. Ranade, a highly reputed Indian scholar considers the unison of the Brahman [the highest abstract reality ever conjured by human mind] and the Atman, the Self, as the completion of this saga of human attempts at decoding the DNA of spirituality, but not before encountering the religious fervour which has undergone successive metamorphoses. Quite often these sorties into the religious realms have genuine human expressions which have gone astray defeating the very purpose for which these were 'created' or 'organised' or founded at various times by the noble and realized souls.

Sri Aurobindo, a glowing epitome of spirituality in the modern era, together with the sublime, all- conquering exhortation of Swami *Vivekananda,* epitomise this trail in the following words:

> Truth they could find and hold
> But not the one Truth
> The highest was to them unknowable.
> By knowing too much, they missed
> The whole to be known.
>
> (Savitri, p 2711)

The vedic tradition is an exception in this context, as it transcends qualifications that religious sects prescribed.

Quite engagingly in this relentless pursuit of perfection, humanity transcended the bound of the philosophical representation of reality called 'spiritualism' and has coveted '*spirituality*' instead, a state of self realization what *Ranade* termed as the 'psychological' in nature.

This exalted state of conception of the self as the Atman, synchronising with that of the supreme reality, the Brahman, was narrowly interpreted by western armchair philosophers as existential freedom. It did find its way in literature, art and other codified human expressions. But, this *Sartorial* or *Heideggarian* Angst was found to be only an 'occasional episode' in the epic pursuit of the Self.

The privileged perception of the philosophers and the religion authorities apart, the clarion call of the *Upanishadic* monism inherits the kinetic power to transform our anxieties and agonies into the blessed state of an everlasting bliss, *Param Ananda,* with its mainstay of self realization *[Atmanam viddhi]. The* thematic refrain of the *Upanishads* could be encapsulated into the four postulates, The *Mahavakyas* which are:

- *That thou Art [Chandogya Upanishad vl. 10.3]*
- *This Atman is Brahman [Mandukya Upanishad v.2]*
- *Consciousness is Brahman [Aitareya Upanishad v.3]*
- *I am Brahman [Brihadaranyaka Upanishad 1.4.20]*

This metaphysical exposition of the self and the Brahman is a seminal spiritual acquisition as it absolves the sinner concept of the human destiny and hitches it to the ennobling realization of being the child of Immortality [Amritasya Putrah]. This psychological state of the self Realization inspires the despondent individual (Vyashti] to identify with the totality (Samashti]. It provides a psychological ballast to human personality. (The term 'psychological' used above is not to be constructed as one that deals with the mental makeup. In the Indian tradition mind [Manas] is considered as one of the senses that man uses to acquire external knowledge. The obvious reference pertains to the psyche, the innermost seat of the consciousness, that illumines the world within. In Savitri, Sri Aurobindo explodes this very misconception about *mind* when he says:

> There is deeper seeing from within
> And when we have left these small purlieus of mind
> A greater vision meets us on the *heights*,
> The luminious wideness of the 'Spirit' gaze
>
> [Book 2 Canto 5]

Here he has very succinctly disposed of the confusion with regard to the meaning of mind, as held in the western thought and instead propounded the one eulogised by the mystic, the *Rishis* of the Vedic lore.

The self realization is the acme of the ascent of human spirit in search of its lietmotif. It means the complete identification of the I (the individual principle) with Self (Atman) and the identification of the Self with the Absolute, culminating in establishing a continuum of I-Self-Absolute (Brahman).

Finally, the metaphysical grandstand together with its spiritual epistemology may put up some formidable difficulties in comprehending 'the sense and essence' of spirituality to all those who approach it through intellection only. However the true seekers of this Supramental state of realization would rather follow what the realized ones have bequeathed us with—to reflect and more importantly, experience, in our lives, be it *Christ* who said *'The Kingdom of Heaven is within You'* or the *Buddha* who taught *'Be light unto yourself'* or the *Vedantic* vision which inspires us to *'Know thyself'-(Atmanam viddhi).*

In fine it could be said that Self realization is the realization that one is heir to the noblest inheritance of immortality, that all existential predicaments are only short episodes in our magnificient march into the realm of spirituality, our permanent destiny. Our soul, our true Self, remains untainted', Supreme in its splendour. In the words of *Wordsworth*–

> Our birth is but a sleep and a forgetting:
> The Soul that rises with us, our life's star
> Had hath elsewhere its setting,
> And cometh from afar:
> Not in entire forgetfulness,
> But trailing clouds of glory do we come
> From God, who is our home

The import of what has been stated is to underscore, to cognise and recognise the final Truth that is achieved only when one dives deep into one's inner world, jettisoning the external trapping and to establish intimacy with one's Self-the all inclusive Spirit, that holds in its embrace, nature, the cosmos, the theos *[God]* and all the individuals, who incarnate divinity.

CHAPTER–2

Our Self: In the Light of Thich Nhat Hanh's Understanding

Dr. Neelam Mehta Bali,
Associate Professor,
M.V. College of Education (Delhi University)

Looking through some philosophy books in a huge bookstore, my eyes stopped on a cover page that showed the picture of a Buddhist monk; the face glowed with compassion and exuded an aura of warmth & peace. The book's title was "Understanding Our Mind" and the Buddhist monk who wrote it was Thich Nhat Hanh. This was my first encounter with the author. The paperback comment "Nhat Hanh focuses on the direct experiences of recognizing and embracing the nature of feelings & perceptions." caught my attention. A quick scan through the book brought me to a beautiful verse quoted in the beginning of chapter six:

> *"The quality of our life*
> *Depends on the quality*
> *Of the seeds*
> *That lie deep in our consciousness"*[1]

The fascination grew stronger and I looked at the next book by the same author, it was titled 'Being Peace'. Again the back page excerpt, cast a spell on me:

"If we are aware of our lifestyle, our way
Of consuming, our way of looking at things,
We will know how to make peace right
In the moment we are alive."[2]

We all feel caught on the spin of our lifestyle, bear the wounds of "life lost in living". But yet cannot discern a way to heal ourselves. A phenomenon which stands substantiated by the growing number of self-help books that one tends to find in bookstores. I am one of those individuals who, suffers the pain of such a wound, is aware of it, looks forward to a healing process which I believe should be innate to my life and not a formulation that is larger than life. As an intellectual and a believer in the perfection of life, I assume that I am being short sighted, there are processes that are integral to my life and my being that can take care of this healing process but I am ignorant of them. This quest for the healing of my being led me to the study of Thich Nhat Hanh's work – largely his book 'Being Peace'. What follows is an account of what I as an individual and a teacher, grasped and tried to visualize as insights that can make education a process of understanding our self.

I would like to begin with the verse on Mindfulness, as in Buddhist thought it appears to be the master key that sets the process of understanding our self, in motion.

"When sunlight shines
It helps all vegetation grow,
When mindfulness shines,
It transforms all mental transformations."[3]

According to Thich Nhat, when mental formations such as anger, fear and anxiety appear in our mind we can invite mindfulness to touch it. Mindfulness is the practice of meditation. We focus on our breath and say, "Breathing in, I know I am angry." Anger and mindfulness come together and depending on the strength of our mindfulness, our anger is recognised, and embraced and if we can nourish our mindfulness then our process of insight meditation would unfold in our mind an understanding of our anger. Mindfulness would reveal anger as part of my own being. Without mindfulness we lose our way, drifting along on waves of suffering. Mindfulness brings us to the crossroad where we can choose the path of our being. Mindfulness is the thought in which we become aware of the five signboards, the five Remembrances - the teachings of Buddha, that helps us to know which direction we want to go, in order to transform ourselves.

Thich Nhat Hanh recalls these Five Remembrances: [4]

1. I am of the nature to grow old. There is no way to escape having ill health.
2. I am of the nature to have ill health. There is no way to escape having ill health.
3. I am of the nature to die. There is no way to escape death.
4. All that is dear to me and everyone I love are of the nature of change. There is no way to escape being separated from them.
5. My actions are my only true belongings. I cannot escape the consequences of my actions. My actions are the ground upon which I stand.

The Buddhist teaching that helps us to know existence of my actions & for that matter of all psychological and physical phenomena (*dharmas*) is called the teaching of Independent Co-Arising. It says that all phenomena that make up what we know as existence are interdependent and mutually condition each other. Chain of interdependent co-arising consists of twelve links (*nidana*), each of which conditions the next. Ignorance (*avidya*) conditions impulses (*sanskara*). Impulses condition consciousness (*vijñana*). Consciousness conditions mind/body, also called name & form (*namarupa*). Mind/

body conditions the six sense organs (*shadayatana*). The six sense organs conditions contact (*sparsha*). Contact conditions feeling (*vedana*). Feeling conditions craving (*trishna*). Craving conditions grasping (*upadana*). Grasping conditions becoming (bhava). Becoming conditions birth (*jati*). And birth conditions old age & death (*jara-maranam*). Interdependent co-arising is the engine that drives the cycle of samsara.[5]

The practice of mindfulness enables us to transform the ignorance (avidya i.e. Absence of understanding) into understanding. If we look deeply, we can get some insight. We can learn to identify the positive and the negative seeds in us. We can learn 'Selective Watering'[6] i.e. we can refrain from watering the negative seeds and practice watering only the positive seeds.

It is important to practice this in ourselves and in our relationships too. We need to practice this for the persons that we care for. It would foster great joy, peace and happiness.

But are there positive seeds in me? How can I be mindful of them, how can I practice? The Buddhist monk says "Life is both dreadful and wonderful. To practice meditation is to be in touch with both aspects."[7] As regards mindfulness he says,

"In everyone there is the capacity to wake up, to understand, and to love. So in ourselves we find Buddha, and we also find Dharma and Sangha."[8]

I: The Basis of Existence

Buddha, Dharma & Sangha have been called the three gems of Buddhism. Buddha nature refers to the "capacity of waking up, of being aware of what is going on in your feelings, in your body, in your perceptions and in the world." Buddha is the awakened one.

In practice, we say "I take refuge in the Buddha", and Thich Nhat Hanh reminds that we should also understand that "The Buddha takes refuge in me". It being so because the Buddha needs us for awakening, understanding and love to be real things and not just concepts...real things that have real effect on life."[9]

According to Thich Nhat Hanh, for Buddha to be real, there must be Buddhakâya, an embodiment of awakened activity. "When we realise awakening, when we are understanding and loving each of us in a Buddhakâya."[10]

The existence of Buddha is inseparably linked with the existence of *Dharma*. "Dharma is the way of understanding and love. *Dharmkaya* just means the teaching of Buddha, the way to realize understanding and love." According to Thich Nhat, in later Buddhism, Dharma came to be understood as "Something like the ontological ground of being"[11]. Hence I assume that anything that inspires understanding and love, that invokes the Buddha, that awakens one to the Buddha in oneself, and makes one smile, is the embodiment of Dharma, i.e. is the Dharmakaya. In other words, it shows you the path of being i.e. the path of Dharma.

Making explicit, the relationship between the existence of Buddha nature and Dharma, Thich Nhat says:

"Anything that can help you wake up has Buddha nature. When I am alone and a bird calls me, I return to myself, I breathe, and I smile, and sometimes it calls me once more...people who are awake see the manifestation of the Dharma in everything. A pebble, a bamboo tree, the cry of a baby, anything can be the voice of the Dharma calling."[12]

Reflecting on the Dharmakaya, i.e. the embodiment of Dharma, Thich Nhat explains, "You cannot use words to describe Dharmakaya. Reality, the Ultimate Reality, is free from all adjectives, either pure or impure."[13] "Dharmakaya can express itself in just *being*."[14] "We can learn from the oak tree; therefore the oak tree is part of our Dharmakaya. We can learn from anything that is around, that is in us. Everything is preaching the Dharma. Each pebble, each leaf, each flower is preaching the Saddharma."[15]

With simple illustrations of the oak tree, Thich Nhat brings home the point that Mindfulness awakens you to the reality that every being that exists has a role to perform and that role is the core of the existence of that being. The role that constitutes the basis of this existence is also the expression of the relationship of this existence with that which is not this. Hence the non-dual understanding of the self/existence.[16]

In other words, the individual is made of non-individual elements. His simple yet insightful understanding is illustrated with reference to the leaves on a tree.

"Leaves...Yes they are children of the tree, born from the tree, but they are also mothers of the tree. The leaves combine raw sap, water and minerals with sunshine and gas and convert it into a variegated sap that can nourish the tree. In this way the leaves become the mother of the tree."[17]

The leaves are Dharmakaya & their existence is non-dual – is realized only by an awakened one – the Buddha. This example is also suitable to realize the third important Gem of Buddhism viz; Sangha, Each leaf does not exist in itself for itself, It is born by a stem that has borne several other leaves. It is nourished by non-self leaf and it also nourishes non-self leaf. It is a collective existence. It's a Sangha. Thich Nhat states: "The Sangha is the community that lives in harmony and awareness. The Sangha needs a body also. When you are with your family, and you practice smiling, breathing, recognising the Buddha in yourself and your children, then your family becomes a Sangha Kaya. Practice (of mindfulness) is easier if you have a Sangahakaya."[18]

Practicing meditation is practicing mindfulness; it is being awake to reality, understanding its way and loving it. We must practice in a way that removes the barrier between practice and non- practice. We must practice 'engaged Buddhism': It means nurturing Buddhism as a way of life. It means we have to bring awakening (Buddha), understanding (Dharma) and love (Sangha) into our daily lives. When we practice we must pay attention to the quality of Practice.

(II) The Practice of Mindfulness:

In Buddhism, the most basic precept of all is to be aware of what we do., what we are, each minute —mindfulness. They practice of mindfulness consists of being aware of

i) The form i.e. our body

ii) Feelings

iii) Perceptions

iv) Formations

v) Consciousness

The practice of meditation can be experienced only in a joyful mood. We must be at ease and be able to smile to undertake meditation. The practice is initiated with the bell of Mindfulness—the voice of the Buddha calling us back to ourselves. In a meditation centre it may be bell invited by a bell master. And in the individual practice it may be the bell in the beginning, and later it may be the any sound that may initiate mindfulness. It may be the sound of a bird or wind. In yet advanced practice the Buddha may come calling us in different forms.

"After mastering the practice to meditate with sound, we can move on to practice with forms. The sunlight coming from your window is also a calling from Dharamkaya for the Budhkaya be and also for the Sanghkaya to be real "[19]

How does the Buddhakaya come to be real?

First, we need to stop the invasion of feeling and thoughts, which deplete our strength in meditation, cultivate the capacity, the power of concentration.

"Calming, smiling, present moment, wonderful moment", reciting this or counting breathing in one, out one; breathing in two, out two;... these or any other technique is used to achieve a two-fold purpose, *one, STOP*– the dispersion of awareness and *two, engagement to achieve concentration* of one subject. According to Thich Nhat,

"Stop and look, that's meditation, insight meditation. Insight means you have a vision, an insight into reality .Stopping is able to see seeing helps to stop. The two are one."[20] He further adds, "Sit there, stop, be yourself first and begin from there, that is the meaning of meditation."[21]

The process is not a simple one, it's a challenge, because according to Thich Nhat, "meditation involves becoming awake of our perception and looking deeply into the natureof our perception." He says "during meditation we have to be something ; and something is what is going on in your body, in your mind, in your feelings and in the world."[22]

His advice is that we should have a good perception of everything to see its Buddha nature and its function as a Dharma teacher His assertion is :

"Perceptions are important for our wellbeing for our peace. Perceptions should be free from emotions and ignorance free from illusion."[23]

Emotions create illusions, thus keeping us from understanding the reality; in other words, we remain ignorant. Hence it is important for us to (become) practice mindfulness and become aware of our emotions. "When we get angry, we have to produce awareness: " I am angry, Anger is in me, I am anger " It is important to become aware that anger and irritation are destructive expression of energy. " We cannot destroy the energy; we can convert only convert it into a more constructive energy"[24]

Forgiveness is a constructive energy Understanding is a constructive energy. " We must transform the destructive energy into constructive energy " Pursuit of insight meditation reveals that ,sometime, somewhere you take something to be truth. If you cling to it so much ,when the truth comes in person and knocks at your door, you will not open it"[25]

One need to recognize that " for things to reveal themselves to ask , we need to be ready to abandon our views about them."[26] According to Thich Nhat , The Buddhist way of understanding is always letting go of our views and knowledge in order to transcend. "You have to be able to transcend your knowledge the way people climb a ladder."[27]

Letting go of our views, beliefs and knowledge facilitates the process of our becoming aware of and awake to the Buddha nature and Dharma of the objects of our perception, as they are, in our present moment experience of them and with them. It awakens us to the reality of that object and the harmony that we can or do share with it here and now. It becomes a moment of practice and meditation. In this present moment of practice we get back to a clearer awareness of our self and a clearer understanding of reality, which infuses greater strengths (in understanding) and love and compassion. It equips us with enhanced capacity to reintegrate into society. Meditation invokes the Buddha, Dharma & the Sangha in greater strides. It enables us to resist a way of life that makes us lose ourselves.

The moot point however is that how does one let go of one's beliefs and knowledge, when that is what one seems to be accumulating and hoarding all through one's life. But behold and recall the Five Remembrances that the Buddha pronounced, which in essence, reiterate the ever inescapable reality of ageing, ill health, death, changing nature of individuals whom we love and of one's actions being one's only true belonging. These remembrances refurbish the foundations of Buddha, Dharma & Sangha, the Three-Fold vision which transports you to the portal of mindfulness, with greater capacity to concentrate, understand and let go or perhaps let go and stronger understanding and greater compassion. It is difficult to say what comes before and what comes after, but perhaps the twin phenomena stand poised together in a wake up moment of mindfulness.

The turning point of the wake up moment is precisely the moment of becoming aware of the Dharmakaya in the field of perception. The Dharmakaya invokes clearer and stronger understanding; and we "walk in a way that we only print peace and serenity on earth"[28]. When not in practice we never have time to look at each other, even those whom we love and the practice of mindfulness gifts us the beautiful opportunity to openly appreciate everyone around us, including our family in our own household. "When you understand, you love. And when you love, you naturally... relieve suffering"[29].

Thich Nhat's compassionate smile seems to say, "It is really beautiful to begin the day by being a Buddha. Each time we feel ourselves about to leave our Buddha, we can sit and breathe, until we return to our true self"[30]. When we are alive to the present moment, here and now, we have sovereignty over ourselves and that makes us happy and so we smile. "If we are aware, we can change the course of things. If we are aware of our lifestyle, our way of consuming, of looking at things, we will know how to make peace right in the moment we are alive, the Present Moment"[31].

References

1. Thich Nhat Hanh, Understanding Our Mind, Harper Collins Publisher India a joint venture with the India Today Group, New Delhi 2006 Edition, Pg 45
2. Thich Nhat Hanh, Being Peace, Full Circle, 2007 Edition, New Delhi, Pg 65
3. Thich Nhat Hanh, Understanding Our Mind, Pg 127
4. Thich Nhat Hanh, Understanding Our Mind, Pg 118
5. Thich Nhat Hanh, Understanding Our Mind, Pg 87
6. Thich Nhat Hanh, Understanding Our Mind, Pg 80
7. Thich Nhat Hanh, Being Peace, Pg 4

8. Thich Nhat Hanh, Being Peace, Pg 14
9. Thich Nhat Hanh, Being Peace, Pg 21
10. Thich Nhat Hanh, Being Peace, Pg 23
11. Ibid
12. Thich Nhat Hanh, Being Peace, Pg 24
13. Ibid
14. Thich Nhat Hanh, Being Peace, Pg 25
15. Thich Nhat Hanh, Being Peace, Pg 26
16. Thich Nhat Hanh, Being Peace, Pg 69
17. Thich Nhat Hanh, Being Peace, Pg 47
18. Thich Nhat Hanh, Being Peace, Pg 27
19. Thich Nhat Hanh, Being Peace, Pg 108
20. Thich Nhat Hanh, Being Peace, Pg 109
21. Thich Nhat Hanh, Being Peace, Pg 110-111
22. Thich Nhat Hanh, Being Peace, Pg 39
23. Thich Nhat Hanh, Being Peace, Pg 42
24. Ibid
25. Thich Nhat Hanh, Being Peace, Pg 43
26. Thich Nhat Hanh, Being Peace, Pg 42
27. Thich Nhat Hanh, Being Peace, Pg 43
28. Thich Nhat Hanh, Being Peace, Pg 111
29. Thich Nhat Hanh, Being Peace, Pg 15
30. Thich Nhat Hanh, Being Peace, Pg 115
31. Thich Nhat Hanh, Being Peace, Pg 65

CHAPTER–3

SPIRITUAL UNITY IN THE THOUGHT OF SRI AUROBINDO: The Very Basis of All Human Education

Arbind Kumar Jha,
Associate Professor,
Central University of Himachal Pradesh

Contemporary global world order and it's political, social, and economic developments may forever transform the way we think about one another and influence the future social reality constructed. Latest acts of brutal capitalism (in some cases), terrorism and hegemonism will certainly have an influential effect on humankind's collective psyche. The concretization of these emerging global issues are especially challenging for educators in general and teacher-educators in particular. As such, many assert that humankind now has a collective responsibility to facilitate the construction of a shared global culture through spiritually oriented educational socialization. This is particularly true for those of us who are professionally committed to educating toward a future existence where peaceful cooperation and planetary citizenship become dominant values that are held in the same high regard as nationalism and individualism are today. Within this context it is critical that we reflectively contemplate what we teach and how we teach regarding these issues.

Education is intrinsically a phenomenon of enkindling the potential spark of perfection enshrined in every human being. Gandhi repeatedly reminds man that he is a higher being than the beast. What distinguishes man from the beast is his dharma consciousness. Any system of education that fails to instill this dharma consciousness, or 'fails to make men of us" is worthless. Modern education is constructive or rather becomes not destructive only when its recipient has evolved spiritually enough to be in total command of his bestial self; i.e. when the material man is managed by the spiritual man. Vivekananda seeks the solutions of all these social and global evils through education based on spiritualism. With this end in view, he feels the dire need of awakening man to his spiritual self wherein, he thinks, lies the very purpose of education. Vivekananda reiterates that religion is the innermost core of education. However, by religion, he does not mean any particular kind of it but its essential character, which is the realization of the divinity already in man. He reminds us time and again that religion does not consist in dogmas or creeds or any set of rituals. To be religious for him means leading life in such a way that we manifest our higher nature, truth, goodness and beauty, in our thoughts, words and deeds. All impulses, thoughts and actions which lead one towards this goal are naturally ennobling and harmonizing, and are ethical and moral in the truest sense. It is in this context that Vivekananda's idea of religion, as the basis of education should be understood. **Why religion forms the very foundation of education becomes clear in his following** words: 'In building up character, in making for everything that is good and great, in bringing peace to others, and peace to one's own self, religion is the highest motive power, and, therefore, ought to be studied from that standpoint. Religion is the manifestation of the divinity already in man. Vivekananda believes that if education with its religious core can invigorate man's faith in his divine nature and the infinite potentialities of the human soul, it is sure to help man become strong, yet tolerant and sympathetic. It will also help man to extend his love and good will beyond the communal, national and racial barriers.

Sri Aurobindo challenges educators to participate in social and spiritual evolution by nurturing the human energy necessary for future progress. He believed that educational institutions are "laboratories of evolution" and teachers are "evolution agents," leaders of the process. Educational curricular activities must be a synthesis of Western positivism with Eastern metaphysics, as well as other globo-local cultural values (Aurobindo, 1995, 2000).

Spiritual Development:

At the outset it's almost impossible to define what spiritual development is. But for all practical purpose, we can say that spiritual development is the process of growing the intrinsic human capacity for self-transcendence, in which the self is embedded in something greater than the self, including the sacred. It is the developmental "engine" that propels the search for connectedness, meaning, purpose and contribution. It is shaped both within and outside of religious traditions, beliefs and practices (Benson et al., 2003).

Freud (1961), who referred to "religion as a universal obsession neurosis," a mere illusion derived from infantile human wishes. On the contrary, Carl Jung noted that religion was "incontestably one of the earliest and most universal expressions of the human mind" (Jung, 1938) and that religion was not only a sociological and historical phenomenon, but also something of considerable personal concern to a great number of individuals. Erikson's stage theory greatly contributed to the faith development theory of James Fowler (1981). For Fowler, faith is universal and can exist within and outside of religious traditions. It's a person's way of responding to transcendent value and power in such a way that the trust in and loyalty to the source of transcendence integrate our identity and give our lives unity and meaning (Fowler, 1981).

Spiritual Development as a Universal Human Process:

Throughout history and across all societies, forms of spirituality have become part of human experience, and it has remained a robust force in life for both individuals and societies, despite numerous predictions of its demise. The notion of spiritual *development* adds an important dimension in its emphasis on process.

Spiritual *development* introduces questions about the nature of spiritual change, transformation, growth, or maturation as well as life phases and stages. For example, Wink and Dillon (2002) argue that spiritual development "demands not only an increase in the depth of a person's awareness of, and search for, spiritual meaning over time, but it also requires an expanded and deeper commitment to engagement in actual spiritual practices.

Interaction between Person and Context

Many conceptualizations of spirituality, particularly in the West, have been highly focused on individual experience and impact. Mattis and Jagers (2001) note that the vast majority of conceptualization and research in the area of spirituality has emphasized the individual "quest," rather than the social and relational context of spiritual development.

Spirituality as a Life-Shaping Force

The preponderance of available research suggests that spirituality has a powerful effect in life.

Sri Aurobindo (1872-1950) was an Indian patriot, philosopher and spiritual master. His written works encompass many areas, from the political and spiritual renaissance of modern India to the intricacies of yoga and the descent of what he called the "Supramental Consciousness". The Integral Yoga of Sri Aurobindo (which he also referred to as synthetic, Supramental, or purna yoga) advocated a total transformation: *physical, vital, mental,* and *spiritual.* In the big picture which he envisioned, moreover, this transformation was for the purpose of not merely individual, but cosmic, salvation. The liberation of the individual was, for Aurobindo, an illusion; what was required was the divinization of the totality of the cosmos, and to literally bring the Kingdom of God on earth. Liberation of the spirit from the cycle of birth and death was not sufficient for the perfection of man's spiritual realization, he felt; rather, the very cells of the body must be brought into contact with the divine light. The rare phenomenon of the divine body (*jyotir maya deha* - "radiant or luminous body") was to be the goal of all yogic endeavours. Until that was achieved, said Aurobindo, realization was not perfect. There are three main stages, a "Triple transformation", in the progression of the Integral Yoga: the Psychic, the Spiritual, and the Supramental. The Psychic Being is the highest part of the emotional being. "Spiritualization" means the uniting of the manifested existence with what is above it."

The spiritual transformation achieves itself and culminates in an upward ascent often repeated by which consciousness fixes itself on a higher plane and from there sees and governs the mind, life and body; it achieves itself also in an increasing descent of the powers of the higher consciousness and knowledge which become more and more the whole normal consciousness and knowledge. A light and power, a knowledge and force are felt which first take possession of the mind and remould it, afterwards of the life part and remould that, finally of the physical consciousness and leave it no longer little but wide and plastic and even infinite. For this new consciousness has itself the nature of infinity: it brings to us the abiding spiritual sense and awareness of the infinite and eternal with a great largeness of the nature and a breaking down of its limitations; immortality becomes no longer a belief or an experience but a normal self-awareness; the close presence of the Divine Being, his rule of this world and of our self and natural members, his force working in us and everywhere, the peace of the infinite, the joy of the infinite are now concrete and constant in the being; in all sights and forms one sees the Eternal, the Reality, in all sounds one ears it, in all touch one feels it; there is nothing else but its forms and personalities and manifestations; the joy or adoration of the heart, the embrace of all existence, the unity of the spirit are abiding realities. The consciousness of the mental creature is turning or has been already turned wholly into the consciousness of the spiritual being."

Integral education for the growth of the soul

Accordingly, Aurobindo conceived of education as an instrument for the real working of the spirit in the mind and body of the individual and the nation. He thought of education that for the individual will make its one central object the growth of the soul and its powers and possibilities, for the nation will keep first in view the preservation, strengthening and enrichment of the nation—soul and its Dharma (virtue) and raise both into powers of the life and ascending mind and soul of humanity. And at no time will it lose sight of man's highest object, the awakening and development of his spiritual being. A concept underlying the true and living integral education.

Integrality of education is conceived as a process of organic growth, and the way in which various faculties could be developed and integrated is dependent upon each child's inclination, rhythm of progression and law of development, Swabhava (inherent disposition) and Swadharma (inner nature). Integral education is not conceived as a juxtaposition of a number of subjects and even juxtaposition of varieties of faculties. The idea is to provide facilities for varieties of faculties, varieties of subjects and various combinations of pursuits of Knowledge, Power, Harmony and Skill in works. These faculties are so provided that they could be made use of by each student and the teacher so that a natural process of harmonious development could be encouraged.

The psychic and spiritual education

Sri Aurobindo also speaks of mental and psychic education, but his real interest is in a still higher stage, which according to him is spiritual or supra-mental education. This does not imply the annihilation of the individual but his enrichment through contact with the Absolute. The spiritual stage transcends the mental and the psychic stage. The justification for psychic and spiritual education rests upon three important considerations: a) education should provide to the individual a steady exploration of something that is inmost in the psychological complexity of human consciousness; (b) the most important question of human life is to consider the aim of human life and the aim of one's own life and one's own position and the role in the society; and this question can best be answered only when the psychic and spiritual domains are explored and when one is enabled to develop psychic and spiritual faculties of knowledge; and (c) the contemporary crisis of humanity has arisen because of the disbalancement between the material advancement on the one hand and inadequate spiritual progression. If, therefore, this crisis has to be met, development of psychic and spiritual consciousness should be fostered. Sri Aurobindo tries to draw a distinction between psychic and spiritual in the following terms. At the life of psychic life, the individual feels an unbroken continuity in the world of forms and sees level as an immortal function in endless time and limitless space. The spiritual consciousness goes beyond time and space and is an identification with the infinite and the eternal. Sri Aurobindo is expressing the same idea when he says that in psychic life selfishness must be discarded, but in the spiritual life there is no sense of the separate self. He insists that it is not annihilation of the individual but its transformation which is the end of integral education. When man attains such education there is total transformation of matter. He calls it supramental education as it will work, not only upon the consciousness of individual beings, but upon the very substance of which they are built and even upon the physical environment in which they live.

The educational doctrine of Sri Aurobindo is closely linked with his futuristic vision of human destiny which is reflected in his statement: They should be children of the past, possessors of the present, creators of the future. The past is our foundation, the present our material, the future our aim and summit (Aurobindo, 1990, p.12). Aurobindo's (1971) visionary mystic mind articulated a concept of life which was unique since he conceived of it as a lavish and manifold opportunity given us to discover, realize, express the Divine and accordingly, visualized a system of education which would help expression of unrealized potentialities, in line with his concept of life. This called for a creative vision and an extraordinary adventure. For him human destiny is an ascent towards the supermind, towards realization of the Godhead and his philosophy of education provides a forceful and resilient framework to attain this goal.

The Triple Transformation of the Individual

Sri Aurobindo's argues that Man is born an ignorant, divided, conflicted being; a product of the original inconscience (i.e. unconsciousness,) inherent in Matter that he evolved out of. As a result, he does not know the nature of Reality, including its source and purpose; his own nature, including the parts and integration of his being; what purpose he serves, and what his individual and spiritual potential is, amongst others. In addition, he experiences life through division and conflict, including his relationship with others, and his divided view of spirit and life.

To overcome these limitations, Man must embark on a process of self-discovery in which he uncovers his Divine nature. To that end, he undertakes a three-step process, which he calls the Triple Transformation.

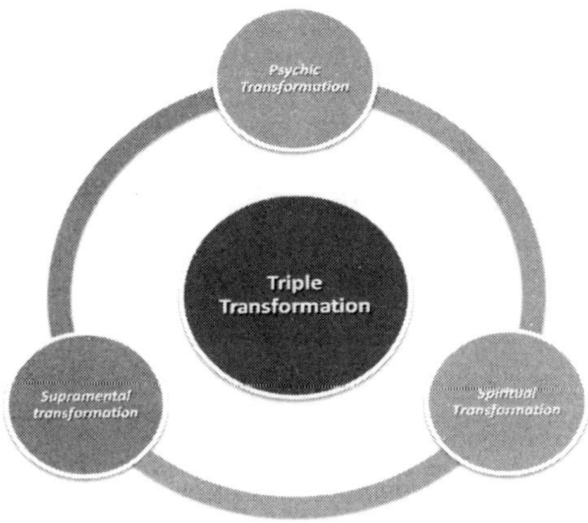

(1) *Psychic Transformation* — The first of the three stages is a movement within, away from the surface of life, to the depths, culminating in the discovery of his Psychic Being (the evolving soul). From that experience, he sees the oneness and unity of creation, and the harmony of all opposites experienced in life. As a result, he begins to shed his essential Ignorance born of creation. He also experiences his true individual nature, shedding his ego and sense of separateness from other and life. He also begins to glean his true individual purpose, as well as his universal and transcendent purpose in life. He comes in touch with an inner Guide that constantly indicates what actions to take and what to avoid. As a result of connecting to the transcendent

divine, he experiences a deep pleasure and bliss, causing him to want to surrender to the Divine Will and Intent.

(2) *Spiritual Transformation*— As a result of making the psychic change, his mind expands and he experiences knowledge not through the hard churning of thought, but through light, intuition, and revelation of knowledge, culminating in supramental perception. Light enters from the heights and begins to transmute various parts of his being.

(3) *Supramental transformation* — After making the psychic and spiritual change, he makes the supramental and most radical change. Sri Aurobindo says the mind cannot easily perceive this possibility, as it goes beyond past spiritual principles and experiences. It is basically a complete transformation of the mind, the heart, the emotions, and the physical body. Consciousness and Force are reintegrated in the being that were lost in the involution of consciousness from an infinite Reality that began in creation as matter. He also has ultimate knowledge that is matched by a power for its effectuation. Thus, Knowledge and Will become fused and one. Whatever he perceives is able to manifest as a reality, reflecting that same power in the original Reality and Being from out of which the universe manifest. At that point, he has the Vision of Brahman that perceives the integral unity of spirit and Life. That spirit is the source of life, and that life is a manifestation of spirit in an ongoing, endless, integral process. The supramental transformation culminates in the change in the very cells of the body, ushering in a new form of human, devoid of the functioning it now exhibits, replaced by their spiritual equivalents. It is the ultimate transformational change. At that point, a Gnostic being is fully realized, as is a collective, Divine Life on earth.

The Evolving Soul (Psychic Being)

Sri Aurobindo indicated that his greatest discovery was the existence of a Psychic Being (i.e. an Evolving Soul) within that is the essence of our spiritual selves. If we forge our way into the deepest parts of our being the Subliminal realm, we will come upon a Personal Evolving Soul. From this Psychic Being we can overcome the limits of consciousness of the individual human. From there we perceive our true nature and essence; we become more aware of our surroundings; we become one with others and life; we experience an inner Guide that influences to move in the right direction and catches our negative propensities as they arise on the surface; we come in touch with our universal nature; we come in touch with the transcendent reality and spiritual Force; we overcome the limits of time, bringing timelessness into time; and evoke the powers of the Infinite into this finite existence, to name several. Also when we plunge within and touch the evolving soul, we move up in consciousness above mind to spiritual mind of illumination, intuition, revelation, and (supramental) truth consciousness. It should also be noted that this psychic entity is itself evolving, as it enters the person's whose experience it believes it can benefit from, extracts the essence of that person's experience, and then moves on to the next birth until it is fulfilled in its journey through space and time. The connection to the evolving soul is thus the key to the evolution from this the human side, as from there we overcome the inherent Ignorance, division, dualities, and suffering of Man, enabling him to fulfill his human aspiration of God, freedom, joy, and immortality. (From the spiritual side, it is the descending Supramental Force that enables the progress of life to its ultimate capacity. The two together, the connection to the Psychic Being and the surrender to the descending (supramental) Force are the keys to the evolution and transformation of the individual, humanity, and life in the universe.)

Aurobindo's vision of the future is connected to our understanding of previous evolutionary stages, present state of existence and the notion of monism- Absolute Reality. He describes evolution as an eternal process with a universal energy causing a dialectical interaction because of our spiritual descent into the world, resulting in an evolutionary assent of the human psyche. The Aurobindoian idea being that involution is the incarnation of the divine on earth through decent into the human psyche. Within this context, Aurobindo asserts that planetary evolution has resulted in the creation of four distinct yet unified earthly realms with a corresponding reality: Material realm (physical reality), life realm (biological reality), intellectual realm (psyche-social reality), and metaphysical realm (higher consciousness-spiritual reality). Each earthly realm has a discernable evolutionary direction of the psyche's development and elevated appearance of the consciousness (Aurobindo, 1974a, 1974b, 1998b; Bruteau, 1974; Combs, 1996; Vrekhem, 1998).

Aurobindo's theory of evolution states that within the four earthly realms seven evolutionary states of psyche (mind), with distinctive degrees of consciousness more elevated than the previous level, have appeared: *Physical mind* is the most basic state of the brain producing elemental consciousness. *Vital mind* is the state of mind with a level of consciousness associated with meta-cognition and affective modes of thinking. *Higher mind* is an important transitional stage of evolution. It is a transitional state between base biological mind and that of reflective knowing (higher consciousness). *Illuminated mind* is a more complex level of consciousness that has characteristics of intuitive knowing and producing visionary thinking. *Intuitive mind* is a distinct state of mind and consciousness empowered by a perceptive awareness of Absolute Reality. This degree of consciousness is found manifested in extraordinary persons endowed with innovative insights and a novel sense of relevance regarding the future human evolution. *Over mind* is the next transitional state of mind. It is characterized by a transcendental level of consciousness and the cognitive ability for integrative thinking, holistic knowing and mystical insight. Accordingly, in our age a few individuals have emerged revealing this level of evolution. Those who have reached this evolutionary state are the pathfinders for future human evolution and advancing global-unity. *Supramind* (that is Supermind) is the future highest level of psyche. It is a total transformation of the human species into a new breed of life and mind. While all the previous levels of minds are supported solely by physical and psyche realms of realities. Supramind is grounded upon Absolute Reality, the Life Divine. Supramind is the Life Divine fully manifested on Earth. He describes the Supramind as the human psyche bathed in divine energy that totally transforms consciousness and empowers individuals to reconstruct human relations into a new social reality of collective global unity.

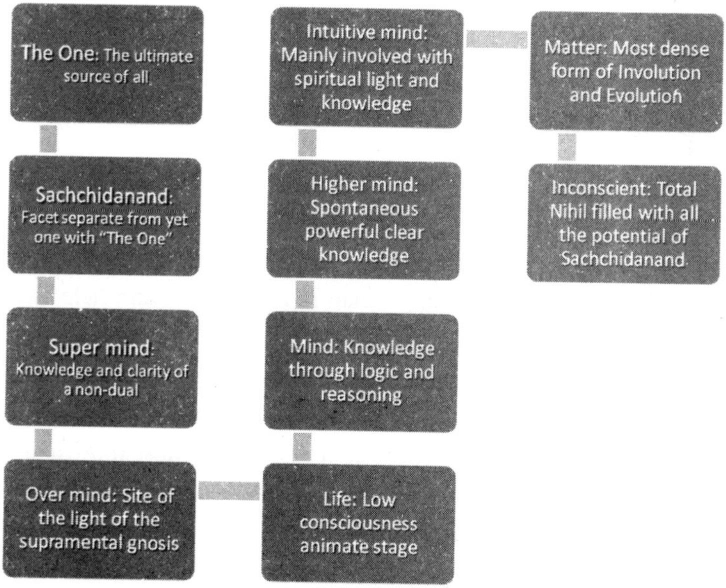

Sri Aurobindo asserts that the notion of Life Divine is not a theory of another worldly reality, strictly an esoteric mysticism. Life Divine is a tangible energy infusing ever-higher expressions of consciousness bringing about greater global social evolution. Supramind results in individuals becoming fully aware of their uniqueness as well as their psyche and social unification with others without perceived contradictions between the two. The complete involution of Life Divine on planet Earth will result in the birth of a new species, "Gnostic being," a being of knowledge, endowed with the capacity to steer future social evolution toward a state of global-unity. The involution of divine spirit into individual's psyche development is driving societies toward increasingly advanced levels of collective consciousness. As a result, societies will continue to evolve toward greater convergence constructing even higher degrees of collective consciousnesses and global social order.

The coming of a spiritual age must be preceded by the appearance of an increasing number of individuals who are no longer satisfied with the normal intellect, vital, and physical existence of man, but perceive that a greater evolution is the real goal of humanity and attempt to effect it in themselves, and to lead others to it, and make it recognized goal of the race. In proportion as they succeed and the degree they carry this evolution, the yet unrealized potentiality, which they represent, will become an actual possibility of the future.

He [Aurobindo] kindles a vision and initiates a work that bears on the whole human situation... man in every mode and field—the thinker [educator], the scientist, no less than the artist and mystic—man individual and man collective—the modern breaker of ground side by side with the heir of the ages...Man is a transitional being, he is not final. The step from man to superman is the most approaching achievement of earth's evolution. It is inevitable because it is at once the intention of the inner spirit and the logic of Nature's process. Humankind must shake off the shackles of slavery to ignorance (Sethna, 1973).

What do We Need?

We need to have Integral Paradigm of Spiritual Education for the purpose of true human education. Integral paradigm is a combination of spiritual attitude, disciplined body work, globo-loco-socio-cultural commitment and development of capacity for spiritual insights. Sri

Aurobindo's Integral education can be used as a potent tool to realize all this.

References

Aurobindo, S. (1974a). *The life divine.* Pondicherry, India: Sri Aurobindo Ashram Press.

Aurobindo, S. (1974b). *The future evolution of man: The divine life upon earth.* Wheaton, IL: Quest Books—The Theosophical Publishing House.

Aurobindo, S. (1985a). *Social evolution towards the ideal of human unity.* Pondicherry, India: Sri Aurobindo Ashram Press.

Aurobindo, S. (1995) (2nd edition). *A new education for a new consciousness.* Pondicherry, India: Sri Aurobindo Ashram Press.

Aurobindo, S. (1998a). *The ideal of human unity.* Pondicherry, India: Sri Aurobindo Ashram Press.

Aurobindo, S. (2000). *Sri Aurobindo and the mother on education.* Twin Lakes, WI: Lotus Press.

Benson, P. L., Roehlkepartain, E. C., & Rude, S. P. (2003). Spiritual development in childhood and adolescence: Toward a field of inquiry. *Applied Developmental Science, 7,* 204–212.

Bruteau, B. (1974). *Evolution toward divinity: Teilhard de Chardin and the Hindu tradition.* Wheaton, ILL: Theosophical Publishing House.

Combs, A. (1996). *The radiance of being: Complexity, chaos, and the evolution of consciousness.* St. Paul, MN: Paragon Books.

Fowler, J. W. (1981). *Stages of faith: The psychology of human development and the quest for meaning.* San Francisco: HarperCollins.

Freud, S. (1961). *The future of an illusion.* London: Hogarth Press and the Institute of Psycho-Analysis.

Jung, C. (1938). *Psychology and religion.* New Haven, CT: Yale University Press.

Mattis, J. S., & Jagers, R. J. (2001). A relational framework for the study of religiosity and spirituality in the lives of African Americans. *Journal of Community Psychology 29,* 519–539.

Sethna, K.D. (1973). Teilhard de Chardin and Sri Aurobindo. A focus on fundamentals. India: Bharatiya Vidya Prakasan.

Vrekehm, G.V. (1998). *Beyond the human species: The Life and work of Sri Aurobindo and the Mother.* St. Paul, MN: Paragon House.

Wink, P., & Dillon, M. (2002). Spiritual development across the adult life course: Findings from a longitudinal study. *Journal of Adult Development, 9,* 79–94.

CHAPTER–4

ADVAITA VEDANTA OF SANKARA

Dr. Reena Kannojiya,
Assistant Professor,
Department of Philosophy,
Miranda House,
University of Delhi,

Introduction

Philosophy is a discipline which plays vital role in developing all other social sciences by bridging the gaps between concepts. Its involvement is essential in terms of ideas that develop out of wisdom by following method of critical inquiry. Hence in generalising particular idea it is necessary to pass it through wisdom, ideologies and critical inquiry. Education is the field which involves all these three stages of philosophy in acquiring or imparting knowledge. Education utilizes all the forms of philosophy as wisdom, ideas and critical inquiry in developing particular point of view which in turn helps in developing a thought or tradition. When these ideologies subjected to critical inquiry then various kinds of beliefs and faith shapes up in different traditions of thought, systems or religions. Education is one of the main medium which propagates idea, thought, principle or fact in form of knowledge that further helps in reformulating or revisiting to the thought or idea so that it could discover new principles or theories. In ancient times education was not imparted by establishing institutions but to those who were curious to know about the phenomenon of this world and beyond this world. Gurus (teachers) taught their disciples by making sit near to them through conversations, dialogue or by oral recitation of verses from the Hindu scriptures. In this manner Hindu tradition passes knowledge from one generation to other in form of verbal testimony. The Hindu scriptures are considered to be infallible as these words are considered to be of trustworthy person. Furthermore, the provided eternal knowledge in Hindu scripture is complex and unsystematic due to which it has been interpreted in different ways and thoughts by various scholars. The difference in thoughts, ideas and ways give rise to different schools of thought, systems, traditions, sects and religions. Moreover, it also reflects difference in understanding, beliefs and faiths. In this way different schools of thought come into existence and made an effort of propounding their teachings in order to provide answers of all those enquires which are pondering in human mind from time immemorial. Every school of thought tries to establish their knowledge which they had realised out of their experience, observation and knowledge. Successively, Indian philosophy has various schools of thought viz., *Charvak, Nyaya, Viseshika, Sankhya, Yoga, Mimansa, Vedanta, Advaita Vedanta.* Each and every school of thought tries to expound and propound their particular ideas, beliefs and thoughts to educate people about the world process. In this chapter Advaita Vedanta of Sankara is emphasised and analysed in brief as a matter of education.

Advaita Vedanta of Sankara:

Advaita Vedanta is a prominent sub-school of Vedanta in Hindu philosophy. There are other sub-schools of Vedanta viz. Dvaita (dualism) and Vishishtadvaita (qualified non-dualism). In comparison to other sub-schools of Vedanta, Advaita Vedanta is the monistic system of thought because it believes in the identity of Self *(Atman)* and Whole *(Brahman).* The non dualism of advaita is one of the major parameter that defines *Brahman as* the source of everything, the *Atman,* the Self and the relation between *Brahman* and *Atman.* The non-dualistic attitude of advaita Philosophy explores Upanishads for these issues from various dimensions and teaches the complete identity between *Atman* and *Brahman* by deriving essential relationship between two. Other vedantic traditions approach to the problem regarding metaphysical reality in different ways.

Sankaracarya (788-820AD) is the most pre-eminent and dynamic propagator or teacher of the advaita school of Vedanta. Sankara is best known as a commentator of *Vedantic* aphorisms, which includes commentaries mainly on *Upanishads, Bhagavadgita,* and *Brahmasutra Bhasya.* These are collectively known as *Prasthana-trayi.*

Sankara was born in a small village Kaladi of Kerala, which is situated in southern region of India. There is a popular story regarding his birth that lord Siva appears in the dream of his parents and gave them a choice over one son who would be short-lived but having most renowned intellectual philosophical ability and many who would be of mediocre aptitudes. Hence, their parents opted for short-lived and intelligent child. So, Sankara was born and lived his life as it was predicted. His life span did not exceed more than thirty two years.

During his life he travelled across India at various holy places and founded four monasteries at *Kanchi, Kasi, Puri,* and *Dwarka.* These monasteries are represented in table below corresponding to each *mahavakya:*

While travelling across India he met with his Guru Govindpada. He instructed Sankara to expound the philosophy of *Vedanta* through commentaries on the principal Hindu scriptures viz., the *Upanishads,* the *Brahmsutras,* and the *Gita.*

The *Upanishads* are the concluding parts of the *Vedas.* Hence, they are also known as *Vedanta.* "There is no unanimity among the scholars regarding the exact date and number of the *Upanishads.* Some

Sishya	Matha	Mahavakya	Veda
Hastamalakacarya	Govardhana Pitham	*Prajnanam Brahman* (*Brahman is* knowledge)	Rigveda
Suresvaracarya	Sarada Pitham	*Aham Brahmasmi* (I am *Brahman)*	Yajurveda
Padmapadacarya	Dvaraka Pitham	*Tattvamasi* (That thou art)	Samaveda
Totakacarya	Jyotirmatha Pitham	*Ayamatma Brahma* (This *Atman is Brahman)*	Atharveda

Table 1: Representing four monasteries founded by Sankara.

says that there were one hundred and fifty; others say that there were one hundred and eight as mentioned in *Muktikopanishad,* which is a work, belongs to the tradition of *Yajur-Veda.*"[1]

Out of these ***Upanishads*** only eleven are known as major ***Upanishads*** on which Sankara wrote commentaries. These eleven are: *Aitareya, Taittiriya, Chandogya, Brihadaranyaka, Mundaka, Mandukya, Act, Kena, Katha, Prasna* and *Svetasvatara.*[2] The word *'Upanishad' is* a combination of two words 'Upa' and 'Ni'. 'Upa' means nearness or quickness. Ni' means certainty. 'Upa' and `Ni' are the prefixes to the root 'sad'. The root 'sad' has two meanings:

- to attain
- to loosen or destroy.

In this way, the word *'Upanishad'* has been interpreted in two ways. It is the knowledge by means of which the ignorance is quickly and completely destroyed, because it is considered that ignorance is the cause of attachment with the world. Or it is the knowledge by means of which one can quickly attain the Supreme Being, *Brahman.*[3] *Upanishads* are in the main concern with what is called spiritual knowledge or knowledge of the Spirit, as it is distinguished from knowledge of matter or of the material world. The *Upanishads* are in short an inquiry into the ultimate truth that leads to eternal peace and immortality.

Bhagwad Gita is the sacred book of *Sanatana dharma.* Principally the *Bhagwad Gita* and the *Brahmasutras* did the reformulation of *Vedanta.* The date and composition of the *Gita* has been much debated. Despite the fact that interpolation and additions were made to it between 200B.C. and 200 A.D., the period of composition of the *Mahabharata* should be deemed to have been basically completed by 200 B.C[4] The *Bhagwad Gita, Upanishads, Brahmavidya* and *Yogasastra* constitutes the ideal focus of the *Mahabharata.* The connection of *Bhagwad Gita* with the *Upanishads is* close. Sri Krishna himself figures in the *Chandogya Upanishad,* and the doctrine, which was taught him there, is recapitulated in the *Bhagwad Gita,* and other diverse teachings of the *Upanishads* relating to *Brahman* and *Atman.* The ultimate analysis of the *Bhagwad Gita* reconciles *karma* and *jnana* in terms of *bhakti* and its ultimate term is the personal *isvara (Purusottama)* rather than the neuter *Brahman.* It is the incarnation of the personal God who without directly fighting holds the balance in the struggle of right and wrong around which the story of the *Mahabharata is* woven. The main teaching of *Bhagwad Gita is Nishkama karma* i.e. to perform action without attachment with external world. It comprises of total eighteen chapters.

The *Brahmasutra* of *Badarayana* systematizes the *Upanishadic* teachings and commentaries written on these *sutras* by many subsequent writers among whom Sankaracarya is well known. It is regarded as *Nyaya prasthana,* because it sets forth the teaching of *Vedanta* in logical order. The *Brahmasutra* have four *adhyayas* with four *padas* in each. The major issues of discussion in the *Brahmasutra* are:

1. The nature of creation and the first cause.
2. The relationship between the supreme spirit and the individual.
3. The role of work and knowledge in relation to salvation.[5]

These commentaries called as *Bhashyas* and sub-commentaries known as *Varttikas, Tikas* and *Tippanis.* With this he also commented on the *Adhyatmapatala* of the *Apastamba sutras,* and on *vyasa's bhashya* to patanjah's *yoga sutras.*

With writing commentaries he also accepted philosophical tradition of debating and participated in various debates with the debaters or profounder of other traditions so that there philosophical ideas can be established by winning over the debate with opposition school of thought. The defeated disciple of the school surrenders before the winner and get converted to the winning tradition. As there was the tradition that the loser will became the disciple of winner. Thus, he debated with various philosophers of Buddhist tradition, *Sankhya,* and kumarila Bhatt who is the foremost proponent of the *purva mimamsa* but as he was on deathbed so his disciple Visvarupa took forward the debate with Sankara. Visvarupa is identified as Mandana misra. Ultimately, Visvarupa get defeated and after which was ordained as a *sannnyasi* by the name of suresvara. He was to become the most celebrated disciple of Sankara, writing *varttikas* to Sankara's *bhasyas* on the yajurveda Upanishads, in addition to his own independent texts on various subjects.[6]

It is considered that in the end of his life, Sankara went to the Himalayas and disappeared in the cave near *Kedarnath,* which is also pointed out as the site of his *Samadhi.* Other traditions believe that Sankara took last breath at *Karavirpitham* or *Mahur* in *Maharashtra, Trichur* in Kerala or *Kancipuram* in Tamil Nadu. As a student of *Vedanta* Sankara is considered to be inherited the teachings of a lineage of most renowned Gurus such as Govindapada, Gaudapada, and others.

Doctrine of Atman

The concept of *Atman is* widely discussed in Hindu scriptures. The different schools of thought have different views in relation with the conception of *Atman,* but Sankara discloses the mystery regarding this concept on the basis of his commentaries on *Prasthana-trayi.* The nature and status of consciousness in relation with doctrine of *Atman is* discussed by Sankara at the three levels of existence *(sattas)*-

1. *Vyavaharika* (empirical)
2. *Pratibhasika* (maya or illusory or dreaming)
3. *Parmarthika* (absolute)

These levels of existence have not been referred in any of the *Srutis.* Sankara's heritage gave this distinction to him from Nagarjuna to Gaudapada, and from Gaudapada to Sankara. Gaudapada also speaks of three *sattas: Paramarthika, Samvrti* or *Vyavaharika* or *Paratantra* and *Pratibhasika.*[7]

At the *Vyavaharika* level, the phenomenal world is considered or reveals to be real, but it is temporary and called as *Kalpita Satya;* it is transcended and contradicted by the *badhaka jnana* of the *Brahman,* which is due to the effect of *maya* or *avidya* in form of illusion or error *(adhyasa). Pratibhasika* existence is non-existence. It is the realm of illusions. It is *'Kalpita eva'.* It is imagined. The snake over the rope is *Pratibhasika.* Its knowledge is false knowledge, it is self-contradictory, and is contradicted by *badhaka jnana* of the rope. However, both *Pratibhasika* and *Vyavaharika is* the realm of the "lower tier". They are both like transcended, contradicted alike, and ultimately have no reality of their own. As a result one is not able to realize the *Parmarthika* or the true nature of self. *Parmarthika is* the only real existence. It is knowledge that is existence and existence that is knowledge. It is the realm of the non-dual, where there is neither known nor any knower. It is uncontradicted, infinite, beyond time, space, and cause. It is the only real. This is *Para Vidya,* the upper tier, the *Aksara Brahman.* Here question arise that, why *jiva is* not able to reveal the absolute nature of self? This question arises due to the epistemological distinction between subject and object. The distinction of subject and object is based on the experience or a matter of consciousness. According to the *Upanishads* consciousness and experience, cit and *anubhava* are one and the same. Though consciousness by its very nature is undifferentiated, in our day-to-day experience it gets differentiated through the objects, which are presented to it, as a result, that it appears to be many. Experience is one, homogenous, and undifferentiated. So in this manner, the two different words, 'consciousness' and 'experience' refer to one and the same entity in *Upanishadic* tradition but appears to change in phenomenological exploration into consciousness, otherwise called as experience.[8] Thought objects and experience (consciousness) are closely interconnected still it requires separate phenomenological approaches to study them. The *Advaita* theory of consciousness is a solution to the analysis of epistemological and metaphysical issues involved in the problem of self.

In the metaphysical sense, it is considered that beside the mind, the senses and the body, there is the Self or consciousness possess by every human being. "It is like a light of lights"[9], which reveals the presence and absence of objects and makes it possible for us to have knowledge of them, but here it is the subject in contrast with the object that is known but distinguishing it here "as subject not in the sense of 'knower' or `cognized' *(jnata* or *pramata),* but it is the ultimate revealing principle, the transcendental a priori, which itself is not revealed by anything else".[10] So, it means the subject never becomes an object and everything other than consciousness is object. Here, *Advaitins* faces with the dichotomy of consciousness and what-is-other-than consciousness i.e. self and not-self.

The ultimate principle of phenomenal world viz. the Self or consciousness, which is involved in all kinds of activities , cognitive, affective, and conative through the mind, the five senses (ear, nose, tongue, skin, eyes) and five motor organs(hands, feet, tongue, the organ of procreation and evacuation) and the body." It has been described as:

"The highest self in so far as it is limited by its adjuncts viz. the body, the senses and the mind *(mono-buddhi), is* by the ignorant, spoken of as if it were embodied.[12] Accordingly, Sankara said that the self itself, but has been limited by the adjuncts *(upadhis).* Here the *jiva* in its empirical *(vyavahrika)* mode of existence thinks of itself as distinct from the *Atman.* When the *Atman is* associated with the *antahkarna* it is said to be pure awareness or consciousness. "The term *'antahkarna'* signifies the activities of the mind in relation to objects with which it comes in contact. The mind is spoken of as *manas* (mind), *buddhi* (intellect)."[13] Sankara further explains the role of consciousness as an underlying principle behind the process of mind-sense-body. Successively, which reveals the whole world of objects is quoted in the commentary of *Brihadaranyaka Upanishads as* follows:

"The self is called light since it is self-luminous, for, through this light, the self-luminous *Atman,* this aggregate of body and organs sits, goes out, and works as if it were sentient in the same way as a jar shines when it is illumined by the light of the sun.[14]

Further, "The intellect, being transparent and next to the self, easily catches the reflection of the consciousness of the self, next comes the mind, which catches the reflection of consciousness through the intellect then the sense-organs. Thus the self successively illumines with its own consciousness the entire aggregate of the body and the organs."[15]

Thus, the mind is the central organ of the entire conscious life; through which impressions carried by the sense-organ are shaped by the mind into ideas. Further, the mind changes the ideas into resolution of the will *(sankalpa).* When a man directs his *manas* the accomplishment of works, he then accomplish them. The very activity of the *antahkarna* presupposes the presence of external objects. If there are no external objects present to the *antahkarna,* then the mind can have no activities. The mind acts in relation to objects outside of itself.[16]

Sankara also interpreted that the embodied *jiva* using *manas* (mind) along with each of the five sense organs, enjoys the sense objects.[17] With this, the individual self *jiva* is defined as the *'amsa'*, an integral part of the lord. Here Sankara compares the *jiva* to the reflection of the sun in water. On removing the water, the reflected sun, which is a part of the real sun returns to the original and remains as the original sun." The word *'amsa' is* also interpreted by Sankara as being similar to the space delimited by the *upadhis* (adjunct) jar, which is a portion of the all-pervasive outer space. On the destruction of the cause of limitation-jar-it becomes one with the infinite space. Thus, the individual self is an imaginary portion limited by the *upadhis* caused by *avidya.*

The analysis of Sankara's concept of *jiva* makes it clear that the consciousness, that is the self-consciousness of the *jiva is* directly dependent on the activities of the *antahkarna* and the *antahkarna* can activate itself in so far as its comes in contact with external objects, i.e. the world. It means that the jiva and the world are related to each other.

According to Sankara, knowledge is broadly divided into empirical and trans-empirical or transcendental following the basic distinction between self and the not-self. The entire not-self constitutes the empirical realm. The mind, the senses, and the body also are the objects of the external world, i.e. not-self. They can be known through *pramanas* i.e. perception *(pratyaksa),* inference *(anumana),* verbal testimony *(sabda),* analogy *(upamana),* presumption *(arthapatti),* and non-cognition *(anupalabdhi).* The knowledge, which we acquire through these *pramanas, is* the empirical knowledge. But Sankara ultimately believe in the *Sruti* or *sabda,* as they are authoritative in nature. So, *Sruti* or *sabda* as a means of valid knowledge has two fold capacities: it can communicate the facts of the sensible universe and can also enlighten us on supra-sensible truths, whereas other vehicles of knowledge are capable of acquainting us only with the sensible. *Advaita Vedanta* holds that true knowledge has not to be verified by any other knowledge and truth is intrinsically valid and its validity is self-evident. It carries conviction. According to Sankara, the Self can only be known through *Sruti; So Sruti is* the source of trans-empirical knowledge. About the mechanism of knowledge *Advaitins* states that Nescience, which is of the nature of an existent, is the cause of all empirical distinctions. It conceal the Omni-present, intelligent self, and transforms itself in the form of the world of diverse kinds. The reflection of intelligence *(cidabhasa)* which resides in the intellect, there arise *pramanas* which is due to the psychosis of the internal organ *(antahkarana-vrtti).* The *pramanas* on reaching the object of cognition e.g. a pot assumes the form of that object.[19] A psychosis is a transformation of the internal organ, and transformation of the internal organ is intelligible, since the internal organ, like milk etc. has parts. The term psychosis is used by modern psychologists to indicate an abnormal state of mind. But here it is employed to mean a transformation either of the mind or of its cause, nescience. The psychosis connects the cognisor and the object cognized. The same internal organ resides in the body, goes out through the channels of the senses, pervades the object and manifests it. That part of the internal organ which is defined by the body is called ego i.e. the cognisor *(pramata),* that part which connects ego with the object is termed cognitive psychosis i.e. the means of cognition *(pramana);* and that part which pervades the object, assumes the form of the object and invests it with the character of objectness is known as fitness for manifestation *(abhivyakti-yogyata)* i.e. the cognition *(pramiti).*[20]

Psychosis may lead either to valid *(prama)* or false *(aprama)* knowledge. *Prama* or valid knowledge can be unsublated and unestablished by any other means.[21] The knowledge of something which is not contradicted and which is novel is *prama.* Unsublatability and novelty are marks of valid knowledge. *Pramana is* the distinct cause of arriving at valid knowledge. *Pramana is* the instrument *(karana)* of valid knowledge. Therefore, all these *pramanas* are realized by *antahkarna* in the different states of consciousness or experience viz.-waking *(agrat)*, dream *(swapna)* and deep sleep *(susupti)* - and the last one which transcends the three states of experience is called *Turiya* or *'caturtha'*, which means the 'fourth'.[22] Here, it only refers to the real nature of the self or consciousness when it is free from the limitation.

The *2nd* verse of *Mandukya Upanishad* denotes as:

"All this is verily *Brahman*. This *Atman is Brahman*. This *Atman* has four quarters." The word `this' means that, which appears to be real divided into four quarters namely, *Visva* (the waking state), *Taijasa* (dream state), *Prajna (susupti* or the state of dreamless sleep) and *Turiya* which is same as *Brahman* or *Atman*. The four quarters correspond to the three *matras* of 'A U M' and the *amatras* of 'A U M'. A, U and M are the three *matras*. The fourth, which is known as *amatras* or without a letter, has no corresponding to *Turiya*.

The 3rd verse of *Mandukya* refers to the waking state as *bahis-prajna-outward* consciousness. Here by outward looking senses means, all those senses by which we are engaged in outward activity and include the five vital breaths which keep up the life process. The outward consciousness *bahis-prajna* of the waking state is a *ekonavimsatimùkhah,* possessed of nineteen mouths- the five senses of perception and the five organs of action make up ten , the vital forces-prana and the rest- make up five, and (there are) mind (the thinking faculty), intellect, ego and mind-stuff. These mouths are the gates of experiences. Through these aforesaid entrances *Vaisvanarah,* thus constituted enjoys gross objects-viz. sound and the rest. Therefore, he is *sthulabhuk,* an enjoyer of the gross. He is called *Vaisvanarah* because he leads in diverse ways all *(Visva)* beings *(nara)* to their enjoyment. Therefore, in waking *(agrat)* state when we reflect on our consciousness, we find it intentional. It is either the consciousness of intended objects like tree, table and other objects existing in the external world or it may be one's own subjective state like pleasure or pain. The mind and senses which function in this state are the instruments through which *Visva,* experiences all kinds of external 'gross' objects.

The second quarter is explained in 4th verse of *Mandukya* Upanishad as *Taijasa,* whose sphere of activity is the dream state. Sankara in his commentary described the dream state in terms of waking state. The consciousness of the waking state, though it is only a state of mental vibration, is associated with many means, and it appears to be engrossed in external objects and thus, it leaves in the mind the corresponding impressions. Under the impulse of ignorance, desire, and (past) action, that mind, thus possessed of the impressions like a piece of painted canvas, makes its appearance (in the dream state) just as in the waking state, but without any external means. In line with this is statement, '(when he dreams), he takes away a little of (the impressions of) this all-embracing world (the waking state).'[23] In this dream state, this deity (the mind) experiences greatness. The mind is *antah,* internal in relation to the senses; and whose *Prajna* awareness in dream takes the forms of the impressions in that *(antah,* internal) mind is *antah-Prajna* aware of internal objects. He is called *Taijasa* (luminous), since he becomes the witness of the (modes of) cognition that is bereft of objects and appears only as a luminous thing. As *Visva is* dependent on objects, he experiences the (modes of) gross cognition, whereas the awareness that is experienced here consists of mere impressions; hence the enjoyment is subtle. Dream perceptions do not look like memories of the past. They are new creations of the mind.[24] This here implies as a whole that Self is really non-relational though it appears to be relational in these states therefore its intentionality is adventitious and not natural to it, that Yajnavalkya stated as *'asango hi ayampurusah',* i.e. the *Purusa,* which is another name for the Self, is non-relational. *Sruti* drives this point through the illustration of a great fish. Just as a great fish swims from one bank to another of a river without being affected or overwhelmed by the current of water, even so the self moves from the waking state to dream and then back to the waking state without being affected or touched by the objects, gross or subtle as the case may be, in these two states.[25] Sankara maintains that dreams can also prophetic or veridical. In this case tradition argues that the individual's good and bad deeds *(dharma* and *adharma)* actually cause auspicious and inauspicious dreams respectively. Thus, these two dream theories presuppose that there is some principle of moral justice at work in the universe. This principle is, of course, the law of *karma.*

Ethically, *Sankara* following the *Vedic* tradition conceive value in two ways: one as a moral or phenomenal reality i.e. *dharma* and other as a noumenal reality i.e., *Brahman. Brahman is* man's either real or noumenal being that constitute highest value to it, due to the attribute of freedom. *Dharma* on the other hand, is the law of phenomenal actions, experiences and is revealed as a system of prescriptions and prohibitions. *Brahman* has to be known, *dharma* has to be practiced. It is derived by the two distinct sections of *Vedas.* One of them is related to action and prescribes the obligations and prohibitions while other reveals the ultimate truth for knowledge. Here, it should not be supposed that the knowledge of *Brahman* requires the performance of *dharma* or that it is itself an obligation enjoined by the *Vedas.* "*Sankara* here distinguishes sharply between the life of spiritual freedom or philosophical wisdom, on the one hand, and the practical life of morality and religion, on the other. `The knowledge of *dharma* leads to *abhyudaya* or empirical well-being but it depends on the performance of the duties. The knowledge of *Brahman* on the other hand, has for its result *nihsreyasa* or absolute well-being which does not depend on the performance of any actions. When *dharma is* enquired into, it is only an ideal to be realized but not real at the time of enquiry. Its realization depends on human effort. Hence, *Brahman* that is to be enquired into is given as real and being eternal does not depend on human effort."[26]

For *Sankara,* the *dharma is* constituted by both *nihsreyasa* and *abhyudaya.* '*Nihsreyasa is* characterized by freedom from desire, seeking pleasure, and pain. It is beyond the dialectic of action and experience, good and evil. *Abhyudaya,* on the other hand, is of the nature of satisfaction which is necessarily limited in duration, scope and degree. It belongs to a process of seeking, activity, experiencing. If *nihsreyasa is* autonomy, *abhyudaya is* necessarily heteronymous, a binding and tempting chain. To attain *nihsreyasa* it is necessary to retreat from external activity into self-knowledge. This is the path called *nivrtti-laksana dharma. To* gain *abhyudaya* it is necessary to follow the path of virtuous action and religious worship. This is the path called *pravrtti-laksana dharma.*"[27] As stated in *Bhagwad Gitdbhdsya, 'dharma is* that which is the cause of the maintenance or stability of the universe and directly instrumental to the relative and absolute good of living beings.

The third quarter i.e. deep-sleep where, we do not have any dreams at all.[28] Even the mind does not function. The absence of the stream of experiences does not mean the extinction of Consciousness. That is how we are able to recall that experiences of sound sleep and exclaim the next morning that 'I slept well; I did not see anything'. If consciousness faded out in that state, the reminiscent experience would be impossible. It shows that consciousness is a thing apart and is not connected with any of these states. "Since the soul in deep sleep leaves the phenomenal world far behind and becomes one with that whose self is Pure Being, it has for its self Pure Being apart from the phenomenal world"[29].

Let us now consider, the textual description of the state of deep-sleep and the nature of *Prajna i.e.,* sleep-consciousness to see the phenomenological approach to the study of consciousness adopted by the *Mandukya Upanishad* in the 5th verse is quoted as: "That state is deep sleep where the sleeper does not desire any enjoyable thing, and does not see any dream. The third quarter is *Prajna* whose sphere is deep sleep, who remains one and undifferentiated who is a mass of mere consciousness, who is full of bliss, who experiences bliss, and who is the doorway to the experience (of the dream and waking state)".

Advaitins maintains that, deep sleep is not only a conscious experience but also it has phenomenological characteristic of bliss *(ananda). To* justify it, *Advaitins* offer two justifications based on scriptural testimony, one is based on *Mandukya Upanishad,* which claims that the deep sleep is full of the experience of bliss and second is based on *Brihadaranyaka Upanishad* which says that sleep is the experience of highest serenity *(samprasada),* bringing with it greater joy than can be found in the waking or dream states.[30]

The fourth quarter which follows in order has to be stated; hence this is presented (by the *Upanishads)* in *'nantah-Prajnam,* not conscious of internal world' etc.

Since, it (i.e.Turiya) is devoid of every characteristic that can make the use of words possible, it is not describable through words; hence the *(Upanishads)* seeks to indicate Turiya merely through the negation of attitudes. With this, it has been described in 7'h verse of *Mandukya Upanishad as* "that which is not conscious of the internal world, nor conscious of the external world, nor conscious of both the worlds, nor a mass of consciousness, nor conscious , nor unconscious; which is unseen, beyond empirical dealings, beyond the grasp (of the organs of action) uninferable, unthinkable, indescribable; whose valid proof consists in the single belief in the self; in which all phenomena cease, and which is unchanging, auspicious, and non-dual. That is the self, and that is to be known". Since turiya is undifferentiated, "He who attains the supreme goal discards all such objects as name and form and dwells as the embodiment of infinite consciousness and bliss."[31]

So, in this manner *Advaitins* account for the totality of mental functions by distinguishing four aspects of mind: sense-mind (manas); reason-intellect *(buddhi); I*-sense *(ahankar)* and recollection-memory (citta).[32] The sense mind, as its name indicates is the means by which the mind "assimilates and synthesizes sense impressions and thus enables the self to make contact with external objects"[33]. This aspect of mind is associated with the mental condition of doubt or indecision, since it provides the knower with precepts but is incapable of discriminating among them. The decisiveness or certitude which accompanies our perception of objects is thus due to the discriminating aspects of mind, *buddhi.* It is by means of reason that, we discern, judge and understand the data of experience. But, through the processes of sense assimilation and reasoning, we begin to develop a point of self-reference which manifests in terms of the I-senses, i.e. in terms of self-consciousness and the pride of egoism. Finally, the fourth aspect of mind distinguished by *Advaitic* thinkers is recollection. In addition to accounting for the actual experience of memory, recollection also serves to explain the manner in which the effects of past experience, in the form of behavioural, perceptual and intellectual habits or tendencies *(samskar),* make their influence felt in present mental activity.

Advaitins conclude that mind is nothing apart from its various functions, which in turn are merely forms or modes of the modification of consciousness resulting from the association of the self and ignorance. A text of the *Brihadaranyaka Upanishad* says: "Desire, resolve, doubt, faith, want of faith, steadiness, unsteadiness, shame, intelligence and fear- all these are but mind.[34]

Ontologically, in its empirical condition Jiva is encased in five sheaths (kolas), one within the other. Jiva come across first with the gross material sheath, which includes the sheath of food *(annamaya kola),* and then go deeper to more subtle sheaths, which includes sheaths of vital airs *(pranamaya kola),* the mind *(manomaya kola)* and self-consciousness *(vijnanamaya kola),* the last being the causal sheath of joy or bliss *(anandamaya kola).* These three bodies are identified with five sheaths *(kolas)* mentioned in the *Taittiriya Upanishad.* The physical body is identified with the sheath of food, the subtle body with the sheath of vital air, the mind and self-consciousness and the causal body with the sheath of bliss. The relationship between the states, the body and the sheaths may be set forth as follows:

Waking state	Physical body	Sheath of food
Dream-state	Subtle body	Sheaths of vital airs, the mind and self-Consciousness
Deep-sleep state	Causal body	Sheath of bliss

Table 2: Relationship between the states, the body and the sheaths

For Sankara these sheaths, which abounds in bliss, can also by transposition, mean the absolute non-differentiated state of the supreme *Brahman.*[35] In this state the Being that was in formal manifestation of self, attains the state of formless. It is a state of supra-individual order that opens the way to experience the state of absolute non-manifestation. We read: All these creatures go day after day into the *Brahma-world* and yet do not discover it.[36] According to *Upanishads,* an individual foretaste the metaphysical union in *Anandamayakosa* in accordance with his nature that calls to experience the nature in the state of deep-sleep. The second sheath of *Atman is Viihanamayakosas,* it is a state manifested as the light of the intelligent *Brahman* in the higher intellect of man. Sankara declares that the one unmodified *Brahman is* made of a plurality of intellects *(buddhi).* Thus, *Atman* manifests itself through the reflection of its intellect upon the intellect of man. The third sheath is the manifestation of the self in the *Manomayakosa-the* sheath of mind of man. *Manomayakosa* means sheath of mind that belongs to the individual and is made up of the internal faculty of cognition known as *manas,* which is of subtle order. It is sheath that gives rise to the ego-sense *(ahankara)* in the thinking Being and makes aware of one as an individual Being. Thus by means of the mind- sheath in man the *Atman* manifests itself in its individualized and subtle form. The fourth sheath is the manifestation of self as the *Pranamyakosa.* It is consisted of aggregate of the organs of action, perception, and the five *pranas* of the physical constitution, namely, aspiration *(prana),* inspiration *(apana),* the intermediary phase between the preceding ones named as *vyana,* expiration *(udana),* and inner assimilation of food *(samana).*

This fourth envelop together with the *Vijnanamayakosa* and the *Manomayakosa* make up the subtle form *(suksmasarira* or *lingasarira)* of the individual Being. The *Pranamyakosa* indicates the subtle manifestations of *Brahman as* the life-giving principle of the physical nature in man. The fifth sheath is known as *Annamayakosa* refers to the gross or physical part of man that manifested in self. It is realized when attention is concentrated on his body and realized as the whole world is *Brahman.* His body reflects the presence of *Brahman* and also forms part of the formal manifestation of the *Brahman.*

Sankara remarks that *sruti* gives an account of the five sheaths for the purpose of revealing the nature of *Brahman as* the inward self by following a process of eliminating the five sheaths just as rice is extracted from the grain by removing the layers of husk.[38]

In the words of Sankara:

"Brahman is the inmost of all the conditioned selves beginning from the sheath of matter and ending with the sheath of bliss. The Sruti text starts with "etasmat Annarasamayat," etc. with a view to revealing, through knowledge, that Brahman as the indwelling self by following a process of eliminating the five Sheaths in the same way as rice is extracted from the grain that has many husks."[39]

The unity of self and reality resulted in pure being, free from all determinations, indescribable by any concepts, or describable only by negations, and symbolized by words such as 'OM' and by deities. Hence, consciousness and being cannot be separated from each other. When we say, "I am here," we are actually saying, "I am conscious of being here." It means I am conscious of my being. *Sat is chit; chit is sat,* because it is the great freedom that we attain, it is called *bliss-ananda* also, so sat-*chit-ananda is* the Ultimate reality.

Further ontologically, the notion of god according to Sankara in scriptures comes into existence when in his view the *Vedanta* text do not teach or purport one cognition of *Brahman.* In order to solve this difficulty he divide *Brahman* in two forms by making a distinction between the *saguna* (qualified) *Brahman* and the *nirguna* (attributeless) *Brahman.* The former is referred as God *(Isvara).* Sankara's view has been seen from two viewpoints; empirical and absolute. The *sagunabrahman is* real in so far as we look at reality from empirical viewpoint. *Sankara* recognizes only one reality i.e. *Brahman.* Everything else other than *Brahman* whether reason or experience move in the realm of error. The knowledge that we receive either by perception or by inference is all because we identify the Self with the body or with the sense objects. But when we superimpose body, the sense organs and the mind on the Self, endowed with adjuncts the Self becomes the *jiva* and it is the subject of all experiences. This error epistemologically is spoken of as "Superimposition" or "Illusion" *(adhyasa),* and in metaphysical terms it is called as *"Maya" or "Avidya".* *Avidya* gives rise to illusions i.e. superimpositions, whereas from cosmic viewpoint *maya is* a principle of illusions. *Maya is* an activity which is magically creative; it is an erroneous identification which is responsible for creating the world in a magical way. The phenomenal world cannot be said either real or unreal; to the extent world is known to us. Even it cannot be real because it depends on *Brahman.* Therefore, it is refer as, *sadasadvilaksana* because this character belongs to its source, *maya.* Hence, this world is neither real nor unreal so it is known as *mithya* (false). It is *anirvacaniyata-vacana* (inexplicable).

Maya is the source of world but it does not act as a power itself. It is the *Brahman* which uses *maya* (i.elsvara) as a power for evolution of this phenomenal world. *Maya, as* power is inherent in Isvara, and god manifests this power through the empirical world of name and form.[40]

Conclusively, it can be deduced that from an absolute point of view, the *maya is* not a power itself, it has no reality of its own. But from empirical point of view, *maya is* a power of *Brahman.* It acts in relation to *Brahman,* and *Avidya* binds man to *samsara.* According to *Sankara,* man is the creation of a negative *(avidya)* principle. Reality as such is non-dual, and the knowledge *(jnana)* of it liberates man from the negativity of the empirical existence. Liberation for *Sankara is* that state of being in which *maya* or non-being is transcended; it is a state which is beyond all duality.

The creation looks to be real, but it is a false superimposition on the *nirgunbrahman* (non-dual Brahman). Sankara accepts the reality of the *sagunabrahman* on the basis of scripture, but when knowledge springs up, scripture ceases to be valid. Thereby, the validity of the *sagunabrahman* loses its meaning. In fact, there is no creation, as soon as it is realized the consciousness of non-difference arises in us and the whole phenomenon of plurality which springs from wrong knowledge being sublated by perfect knowledge. It shows that the knowledge of *sagunabrahman* comprise of different cognitions, while the knowledge of the *nirgunabrahman is* comprised of one cognition, which is considered as the real. Finally, it could be followed that Sankara did not reject god (Isvara) in practical life so far it is known to us of having a definite form. In this way, empirical realm is an important aspect of *Advaita* in proving the existence of god till perfect knowledge of *Brahman is* realized.

According to *Upanishads* the intrinsic characteristic *(svarupalaksana)* of *Brahman* are expressed in following statements:

'*Brahman is* Truth, Consciousness, Infinite. (Tai.U.II.1.3) *Brahman is* Consciousness, Bliss'. (Br.U.III.9.28)

'Supreme *Brahman is* Being-Consciousness-Bliss'. (N. P.T.U. 1.6)

Upanishads also define *Brahman* by extrinsic characteristics *(tatastha laksana),* which do not inhere it, but differentiate It from all else, such as:

'That from which are the projection, the preservation, and the dissolution of the universe.' (B.S.S.B.I.i.2)

'That from which these beings are born, that by which, when born, they live, that into which (at the time of dissolution) they enter, they merge; seek the knowledge of that. That is *Brahman.'* *(Tai. U.Ill.i)*

'He is the lord of all. He is the knower of all. He is the Inner Controller. He is the source of all; for from him all beings originate and in him they finally disappear.'(Ma.U.VI.)

'All this is *Brahman.'(Ch.U.11.14.1)*

Sruti declares the identity of individuai self and supreme self in form of an individual consciousness and supreme consciousness that sustains and manifests the manifold. This is the sole reality of non dual, non-relational Pure consciousness i.e. *Brahman.* The whole truth reveal through the five sentences of four *Vedas.* Each sentence is called a *'Mahavakya',* whose literal meaning is, 'the great saying'.

Thus we can sum up the notion of self in Sankara's philosophy as explained in five *Mahavakyas. Prajnama Brahman,* Consciousness is *Brahman (Aitareya Upanishads* III.1.3), *Aham Brahmasmi, I* am Brahman (*Brihadaranyaka Upanishad* IV.iii.23), *Tat Tvam asi* , Thou art that *(Chandogya Upanishad VI.8.7), Ayam Atman Brahman,* This *Atman is Brahman (Chandogya Upanishad III 10-14, Taittiriya Upanishad I.1, Brihadaranyaka Upanishad 11.5.19), Sarvam Khalu idam Brahman (Chandogya Upanishad III. 14.1, Mundaka Upanishad* III.13.1).

Advaita Vedanta of Sankara tries to educate people by revealing the fact of non-duality is that the whole world process is an illusion or error for which man performs all kind of malpractices to attain happiness or bliss but in reality the real education lies in the fact that by knowledge, devotion to god and purity of *Atman* can lead to realise the highest *(Brahman)* through the removal and destruction of ignorance, grief, sorrow and impurity of character and action. If this world can follow Sankara's ideology then nobody would get indulge himself in immoral and unethical activities, as this empirical world is considered to be unrealistic and unnecessary. The reality lies in the realisation of *Atman as Brahman,* which is the ultimate state of bliss.

Foot Notes

1. Diwakar, R.R. *Upanishads In Story And Dialogue,* Bombay, Hind Kitabs Ltd., 1950, p.10
2. Nikhilananda, Swami. *The Upanishads,* London, George Allen and Unwin Ltd., Ruskin House, Museum Street, 1949, p.21
3. Chattopadhya, B.K. *The Teachings of the Upanishads,* University of Calcutta, 1952, p.9
4. Pande, G.C. *Life and thought of Sankaracarya,* Delhi, Motilal Banarsidas Pvt. Ltd., 1994, p.137
5. Pande, G. C. *Foundations of Indian Culture,* Delhi, Sundeep Prakashan, Vol. I. p.125
6. *http://www.advaita-vedanta.org/avhp/sankara-life.html* retrieved on *20 July 2010*
7. Mudgal, S.G. *Advaita Of Sankara-A Reappraisal,* Delhi, Motilal Banarsidass, *1975, p.3*
8. Balasubramanian, R. *Phenomenonlogy Of Consciousness,* Series-6, New Delhi, Indian Council of Philosophical Research, 2003, p.1
9. Gmmbhrrananda, Swami. (trans.), *Mundaka Upanishad,* Calcutta, Advaita Ashram, 1978, p.63 (Mu.U.II.ii.9)
10. Balasubramanian, R. *Phenomenology Of Consciousness,* etc., p.6
11. Nikhilananda, Swami. *Self-knowledge,* Chennai, Sri Ramakrishna Math, 2004, p. 56
12. Gambhirananda, Swami. *Brahmasutra-Bhasya,* Calcutta, Advaita Ashram, 1972, pp. 114-115 (V.S.B.1.2.6)
13. Pandit, Motilal. *Sankaras Concept Of Reality, N.* Delhi, Select books publishers and distributors, *1981, p.43*
14. Balasubramanian, *R. Phenomenology Of Consciousness,* etc., *p.8 (Br. U. 4.3.7)* 15 mid. *p.9 (Br. U.4.3.8)*
16. Gambhirananda, Swami. *Brahmasutra-Bhasya,* Calcutta, etc., *pp.402-404 (V.S.B. 2.2.17-18)*
17. Panoli,V. *Gita In Sankara's Own Words,* Calicut, The Mathrubhumi Printing & Publishing Co., *1990, p.243 (BG15.9)*
18. Ibid. *p.241(BG15.7)*
19. Ibid.

20. Ibid. *p.12* 21 mid.
22. Gambhirananda, Swami. *Mandukya Upanishad, 2000,* Calcutta, Advaita Ashrama, *pp.9-10 (Ma.U.2)*
23. Madhvananda, Swami. *The Brihadaranyaka Upanishad,* etc., p.631(Br. U.IV.iii.9)
24. Ibid. p.637 (Br.U.IV.iii.10)
25. Balasubramanian, R. *Phenomenology Of Consciousness,* etc., p.26 *(Br. U.* 4.3.15-16, 18)
26. Pande, G.C. *Life And Thoughts Of Sankaracarya,* Delhi, Motilal Banarsidas, 1994, p.219 (B.S.S.B.1.1.1)
27. Ibid.pp.220-221
28. Gambhirananda, Swami. *Mandukya Upanishad,* Calcutta, Advaita Ashram, 2000, p.15 *(Ma.* U.5)
29. Iyer Venkatarama, M.K. Advaita *Vedanta,* etc., p.122
30. Madhvananda, Swami. *The Brihadaranyaka Upanishad,* etc., p.645 *(Br.* U4.3.15)
31. Indich, William.M. *Consciousness InAdvaita Vedanta,* etc., p.107 *(AB,* 40)
32. Datta, D.M. *The Six Ways OfKnowing,* London, George Allen and Unwin, 1932, p.48 (B.S.S.B, 2.3.3-2)
33. Deutsch, Eliot. Advaita Vedanta- *A Philosophical Reconstruction,* Honolulu, University Press of Hawaii, 1964, p.60
34. Balasubramanian, R. *Advaita Vedanta,* etc., *p.83 (B.S.S.B 1.5.3)*
35. Thibaut, George. (trans.), *Vedanta-Sutra-With The Commentary By Sankaracharya,* Delhi, Motilal Banarasidass, *1998, p.65 (B. S. S.B I.1.12-19)*
36. Deussen, Paul. *Sixty Upanishads Of The Veda,* trans. V.M.Bedekar and G.B.Palsule, N.Delhi, Motilal Banarsidass, 1980, p.178 *(Ch.* U. VII.3.2)
37 Payyappilly, Joseph. *The Concept OfMan In The Advaita Vedanta OfSankara,* Frankfurt, Peter Lang, 2005, pp.337-338
38. Balasubramanian, R. *Advaita Vedanta,* New Delhi, Centre for studies in civilizations, 2000, p.80 *(Tai. U.* 2.2.1)
39. Balasubramanian, R. *Advaita Vedanta,* etc., p.100 *(Tai.* U.2.2.1)
40. Ibid. (V.S.B. 1.4.3)

References

Balasubramanian, R. *Advaita Vedanta,* New Delhi, Centre for studies in civilizations, 2000

Balasubramanian, R. *Phenomenology Of Consciousness,* Series-6, ICPR, New Delhi, Motilal Banarsidass, 2003

Chattopadhya, B. K. *The Teachings of the Upanishads,* University of Calcutta, 1952 Datta, D.M. *The Six Ways Of Knowing,* London, George Allen and Unwin, 1932 Deussen, Paul. Sixty *Upanishads Of The Veda,* trans. V.M.Bedekar and G.B.Palsule, N.Delhi, Motilal Banarsidass, 1980

Deutsch, Eliot. *Advaita Vedanta- A Philosophical Reconstruction,* Honolulu, University Press of Hawaii, 1964

Gambhirananda, Swami. *Brahmasutra-Bhasya,* Calcutta, Advaita Ashram, 1972 Gambhirananda, Swami. *Mandukya Upanishad,* Calcutta, Advaita Ashram, 2000 Indich, William M. *Consciousness In Advaita Vedanta,* Delhi, Motilal Banarsidass, 1980

Iyer Venkatarama, M.K. *Advaita Vedanta,* New York, Asia Publishing House, 1964 Madhvananda, Swami. *The Brihadaranyaka Upanishad,* Almora, Advaita Ashram, 1950

Nikhilananda, Swami. *Self-knowledge,* Chennai, Sri Ramakrishna Math, 2004

Pande, G.C. *Life and thought of Sankaracarya,* Delhi, Motilal Banarsidas Pvt. Ltd., 1994

Pandit, Motilal. *Sankaras Concept Of Reality,* N.Delhi, Select books publishers and distributors, 1981

Panoli,V. *Gita In Sankara's Own Words,* Calicut, The Mathrubhumi Printing & Publishing Co., 1990

Payyappilly, Joseph. *The Concept Of Man In The Advaita Vedanta Of Sankara,* Frankfurt, Peter Lang, 2005

Gambhirananda, Swami. (trans.), *Mundaka Upanishad,* Calcutta, Advaita Ashram, 1978

Diwakar, R.R. *Upanishads In Story And Dialogue,* Bombay, Hind Kitabs Ltd., 1950 Nikhilananda, Swami. *The **Upanishads**,* London, George Allen and Unwin Ltd., Ruskin House, Museum Street, 1949

Thibaut, George. (trans.), *Vedanta-Sutra-With The Commentary By Sankaracharya,* Delhi, Motilal Banarasidass, 1998

CHAPTER–5

YOGA: THE ETERNAL PANACEA

Ms. Savita Sharma,
Advocate,
Supreme Court, Delhi

PART-I

The Universal goal of human aspiration is to attain perennial bliss, which would also mean our release from misery for all time. Perhaps, this is what gives us the most comprehensive definition of Yoga. In fact, this is the end sought to be achieved through the practice of Yoga. The sacred work "Yoga" has been defined in a number of places from different angles by Lord Krishna - 'Yogeshwara' in his spiritual classic 'The Bhagvad Gita' such as "Yogah Karmasu Kaushlam" - Yoga is skill in action (Chapter II, Verse 50); "Samatvam Yoga Uchyate" - Evenness of mind is called Yoga. However, the most remarkable definition is given in Chapter IV, verse 23, where he says that Yoga is '*Dukhasamyoga Viyogam*' - Separation from pain to be eternally established in the lasting perfection. Patanjali in his Yoga Sutras has also set various guidelines for the attainment of this ultimate goal. He defines it (Yoga) as "Chitta-Vritti Nirodha" or the control of the modifications of the mind-stuff. This is a remarkable science designed to restore the man his forgotten identity. Although stress is laid on the control of the mind but it encompasses the entire gamut of the spiritual ascent. Swami Krishnanandaji of the Divine Life Society in his erudite interpretation of the Patanjali's Yoga Sutras, states that "Nothing can be dearer to man than Yoga........ It is a system which we are to accommodate into out own personal and practical day to day life as an art, by which we shall place ourselves in a greater proximity to the situation of ultimate liberation". This necessarily implies that we are far from it. Swami Shivanandaji in his book "Yoga and Realisation" introduces Yoga as concentration of the mind within, by withdrawing it from the objective universe. Its purpose, of course, is to help the Sadhaka to enter into conscious communion with the Lord through Samadhi, which is the ultimate goal of human existence. Underlying all these expositions on Yoga, the emphasis is on the *disciplining of the mind* for the purpose that is hailed by the Vedas and Shastras not merely as a culture of India but as a final destination of the entire human race - the Grand Union.

The reason why it is the mind that is required to be disciplined has to be understood thus - only that which is subtle can pervade and comprehend, what is gross. The Universe which is the object is grosser than our senses which perceive it. Then senses are gosser than subtle energy whic actuates the senses. Finally, that which characterizes the energy and which is more subtle and pervasive is consciousness. Energy subsists in consciousness. Energy works as and when it is willed by consciousness. Thus Absolute Consciousness is that beyond which there is nothing. In fact, 'nothing' is a misnomer because the Absolute is a comprehensive fullness. This objective universe is some kind of an expression or manifestation of this consciousness. However, being circumscribed by space and time it (Universe) is limited. Similarly, human being, objectively inclusive in the universe is a limited individuality existing in a subtle form as Mind, i.e., *Manas Chatushtya - Mana, Buddhi, Chit, Ahamkara.* Mind is the creation or the individualized form of consciousness. Yet, mind by its own peruliar feat causes itself to be limited, assuming itself as apart from existence. Therefore, by a similar feat, it has to revert and get established in its original infinite (limitless) condition which alone can and does exist.

There are several subtle questions that arise here. First, as to what this Yoga, commonly called 'Union' is about? Secondly, what is the nature of this Union? It is only if we know the nature of this Union that the modus operandi can be thought of, for attaining it. Thirdly and finally, what is the real mystery behind this lofty "Union" which makes it 'dearer to man' that anything else. At the bottom of this foray of doubts which are presented before us as psychological difficulties, is our lack of knowledge or rather our ignorance and inability to understand the truth of ourselves and our relationship to the Universe at large. Howsoever thick this veil of ignorance over our psyche may be, it still is not impregnable. This is so because the truth of our 'self' and its relation with the universe are but inseparable aspects of the same reality or truth. And that is why the instrument or method of investigation by which it can be understood has also to be one and the same. It is a matter of common experience that whatever we know we know through mind and there is no second way. It is the mind that is the power or faculty we possess for knowing the existence of external Universe of which we are also a part and also its nature. Mind simultaneously being our internal faculty, also knows the texture of our mental nature. Therefore, it is the mind which is capable of evidencing the inseverability and oneness of the self and the Universe.

Here, there are certain other points for consideration relating to the nature and functioning of the mind which become relevant for the appreciation of Yoga - its methods and practices. Now, there is not doubt that it is mind that is the cause of human knowledge and human action. "Attention" is the function of mind as one pointedness is the quality of attention and 'Activity' is just the property of mind. Therefore, it is in one aspect the organ of perception concerned in receiving sensations from the external world and in the another aspect the organ of direction concerned in guiding the senses of action of work with a view to achieving some object. So the mind in relation to the senses of knowledge is knower and in relation to the senses of action is the actor. Being an organic unity and a basis of sensations it cannot be said to have evolved from matter alone. What then is the other (thing) from which it has evolved or from which it has been created? Creation as such is twofold - objective and subjective. The objective side of creation is the projection of the substance of the world and everything it contains, from the Cosmic Mind. the subjective side consists of the nature of the object as conceived by the perceiver which would differ according to the varied limitations of the individual perceiving minds. The emphasis in the theory of creation is on the phenomenon of perception. When there is perception of an object (i.e., the Universe) by the observer, there has to be the existence of consciousness between the subject and the object. It would mean that if there is no conscious connection between the two, there would be no perception of existence. Therefore, what relates the subject to the object is the consciousness and hence the subject and the object are but only phases of a universal consciousness expressing itself through the Cosmic Mind which in philosophic parlance is known as Hiranyagarbha. The individual mind being essentially inseparable from the cosmic mind would be essentially an expressive entity of consciousness. As an individual mind, limited and conditioned by its psychic structure and modifications, it operates as an instrument or agent of consciousness.

The Absolute or Universal Consciousness is Existence. It never came into existence. It is there and nobody created it. It is there and, therefore, does not require any cause for its creation. It is what it is. This explanation is also some kind of a scientific view which states that no outside intervention is required for Creation. It exists and both the gross Universe and our minds which perceive it are within this Existence. Nothing can be outside it. So, our relationship with things and our conduct in life depends upon the way in which we understand things. Critical to this understanding is our perception (as has been stated earlier) of the world as being outside us. It is this which has caused duality to the way our life is lived. Otherwise, the Absolute - The Brahman is all comprehensive. Full - 'Poorna' and is, therefore, designated as 'that which is' - rising above any individual concept. Anything less than the Absolute can have, at best only a relative existence circumscribed by space and time. It is called relative existence because such existence is dependent on the standpoints of the observing individuals. Its distance (space) and duration (time) would be related to the state of consciousness wherever they are experienced.

The mind thus creates an understanding of world as a phenomena, though mind itself is the creation if we may say so, of the Absolute which also intrinsically encompasses within itself the Universe. Such an understanding or the perception by Mind in viewing the world as being outside leads to another aberration which is more serious in the sense that it entertains the notion of individuality. The very fact of individuality denotes that individuality is not complete. This sense of incompleteness leads to involuntary urge from within to strive to become complete perfect. It is this urge, desire or want which manifests itself as action, as an move towards its fulfillment. This is why there is a constant rush outwards. Action becomes an indispensable part of the individual. Philosophical implication of such action is that there is something towards which the whole universe seems to be gravitating and without which all one does in this world would be meaningless. It is promoting of such action, on determination by mind, that is the ultimate purpose of Yoga. Further, the simultaneous inner quest and the outward expression of mind creates contradiction (which has been discussed earlier) in the function of mind and its properties. Here again it is Yoga that resolves this epistemolgical predicament by bringing about harmony in our inner and outer world. It may not only be relevant but even necessary to understand that disharmony dislocates us internally as we get entangled more and more in the external world. Extrication from it becomes even more difficult because the goals of life having drifted outside get defined by all that is perceived by the senses. It is common experience that what is perceived by senses is far removed from a true insight into the things. Therefore, any action founded on partial knowledge can only lead to unpleasant experience and consequently sorrow as the action would be such by which Truth is deserted. This perhaps is the hidden rationale behind the usage that "little knowledge is dangerous". Not only does action which is divorced from Truth result in sorrow but also action itself causes sorrow. Being produced by the motion of the mind and the senses, it evidently is the process. Process means change and change marks the process as distinct from perfection. And till perfection is attained, actions and reactions from a continuous chain in the metempsychosis, i.e., the continuity of conscious existence associated with some form. This is the greatest grief which has afflicted man. However, since impulse for action is ingrained in human constitution, it is not possible to cease action till human consciousness lasts. Yet such action which is conducive t or brings one closer to Perfection would be commendable as it would bring about cessation of activity itself to finally rest in the pristine Absolute.

The obvious conclusions which follow from above analysis are firstly, that it is the cosmic mind, by ascertaining its notional independence creates the subject and the object in the form of the external Universe (human mind also creates its own world). Secondly, by assuming duality, the mind causes a conceptual atrophy in the Absolute. Thirdly, the diminutive self in the garb of Mind desires to overcomes its imperfection by its effort. Effort defined in terms of mind is acquiring of an understanding of the Absolute. Such an understanding propels action. It is action that becomes an intrinsic impulse of individualized self and it cannot be case off. Yet without cessation of activity restlessness continues. Therefore, mind is caught in the predicament of action and non-action. Fourthly, if the action emanates from the urge to strive for perfection, the dilemma gets resolved automatically. Mind having reached the pinnacle of perfection ceases its activity to rest in peace in its original state of Absolute one pointedness. When the mind fixes itself thus, then it becomes disinterested in the experience of pain ad pleasure resulting from its contact with the world and hence is released from the tyranny of death and desire. Well, this is all the YOGA is about! - a process of the evolution of the finite to the infinite, consciously and deliberately systematized.

Before proceeding to the modes adopted for the practice of Yoga it may be relevant to clarify that mind here is being talked about in the sense of 'Manas Chatushtaya' - Mana, Budhi, Chitta, Ahamkara. Such a mind is subtler than even the subtle principles which preside over the senses because it is the synthesizing agent behind the diverse sense-functions. Freeing itself from the perception of duality and resting as omniscience (all knowing), it becomes a potential condition for the appearance of the Absolute - The Brahman which is the supreme destination of all. The literal meaning of the word 'destination' may raise a doubt that such a process involves a movement but it is only a figurate usage in the sense of attainment of the goal of Brahman. Attainment of Brahman means realization, i.e., knowing the Brahman. It can only be the knowing of the Brahman because there cannot be any literal movement towards it, because there is nothing external to the Absolute. Movement is action but opposed to it, knowledge is Being, i.e., that what is realization. It is 'Existence'. Therefore, it means that Existence is co-extensive with all knowledge and knowledge is consciousness. Nature of the Absolute, it is said is Omnipresent (all-pervading, i.e., one), Omniscient (all knowing) and Omnipotent (all powerful). The Absolute or Brahman is all pervasive because it is subtle. Only that which is subtle can be pervasive above the barriers of Time and Space or any other dimension if there is. It is total awareness since consciousness is co-extensive and knowledge. It is all powerful because omnipotence is corollary of omniscience to the extent one has knowledge, one can have power. In order to have absolute power, complete knowledge is essential and, therefore, knowledge and power go together with Being - "Brahma Brahmaiva Bhawati" - one who knows Brahm becomes Brahm; all pervading, all knowing and all powerful.

A very interesting, rather wornderful proposition which is brought to limelight from the above arduous discussion, is, that all that is required in Yoga and for Yoga is the change in the direction and attitude of Mind from individuality to universality. Man becomes God with a guarantee of no return to mortality. Simple, though this remedy appears to be, it casts but a very very onerous duty of realization on man. Yoga, by its various modes makes possible this realization. Yoga is, thus, the science of life and also its goal.

Section-B

SPIRITUALITY: THE EDUCATIONAL PATHWAY

CHAPTER–6

Spiritual Development Through Education -Swami Vivekananda

Dr. Naraginti Amareswaran,
Researcher,
Dept. of Education, Sri Venkateswara University,
Tirupati-517502, Andhra Pradesh

Dr. S.K. Panneer Selvam,
Assistant Professor,
Dept. of Education, Bharathidasan University,
Tiruchurapalli, Tamil Nadu

Introduction

Sanskrit	**English**
Om Om Om	Om Om Om
Asatho Maa Sath Gamaya	Lead me from unreal to real
Thamaso Maa Jyothir Gamaya	Lead me from darkness to light
Mruthyor Maa Amrutham Gamaya.	Lead me from death to immortality.
Om Shanthi. Shanthi. Shanthi.	Peace, peace, peace is to all. May the entire world be happy?

Swami Vivekananda (1863–1902), a great thinker and reformer of India, embraces education, which for him signifies 'man-making', as the very mission of his life. Vivekananda realizes that mankind is passing through a crisis. The tremendous emphasis on the scientific and mechanical ways of life is fast reducing man to the status of a machine. Moral and religious values are being undermined. The fundamental principles of civilization are being ignored. Conflicts of ideals, manners and habits are pervading the atmosphere. Disregard for everything old is the fashion of the day. Vivekananda seeks the solutions of all these social and global evils through education. With this end in view, he feels the dire need of awakening man to his spiritual self wherein, he thinks, lies the very purpose of education.

Goal of Education

Vivekananda points out that the defect of the present-day education is that it has no definite goal to pursue. A sculptor has a clear idea about what he wants to shape out of the marble block; similarly, a painter knows what he is going to paint. But a teacher, he says, has no clear idea about the goal of his teaching. Swamiji attempts to establish, through his words and deeds, that the end of all education is man making. He prepares the scheme of this man-making education in the light of his over-all philosophy of Vedanta. According to Vedanta, the essence of man lies in his soul, which he possesses in addition to his body and mind. In true with this philosophy, Swamiji defines education as 'the manifestation of the perfection already in man.' The aim of education is to manifest in our lives the perfection, which is the very nature of our inner self. This perfection is the realization of the infinite power which resides in everything and every-where-existence, consciousness and bliss (satchidananda). After understanding the essential nature of this perfection, we should identify it with our inner self. For achieving this, one will have to eliminate one's ego, ignorance and all other false identification, which stand in the way. Meditation, fortified by moral purity and passion for truth, helps man to leave behind the body, the senses, the ego and all other non-self elements, which are perishable. He thus realizes his immortal divine self, which is of the nature of infinite existence, infinite knowledge and infinite bliss.

At this stage, man becomes aware of his self as identical with all other selves of the universe, i.e. different selves as manifestations of the same self. Hence education, in Vivekananda's sense, enables one to comprehend one's self within as the self everywhere. The essential unity of the entire universe is realized through education. Accordingly, man making for Swamiji stands for rousing mans to the awareness of his true self. However, education thus signified does not point towards the development of the soul in isolation from body and mind. We have to remember that basis of Swamiji's philosophy is Advaita which preaches unity in diversity. Therefore, man making for him means a harmonious development of the body, mind and soul. Education for him means that process by which character is formed, strength of mind is increased, and intellect is sharpened, as a result of which one can stand on one's own feet.

Education of the Masses

According to Swami Vivekananda a nation's progress is depending on the spread of education among the masses. The bane of India's progress is that the whole education and intelligence of the land became the monopoly of a handful of men. Unless and until we care for the spread of education among the masses^ no progress will be achieved in this country. Priest power and foreign rule have exploited the poor people to such an extent that they don't even think they are human beings. In a sad situation like this we have to open their eyes and make them see what is happening in the world around. "Our duty is to put the ideas into their heads, they will do the rest." He contended.

Swami blamed 'the cruel society which is interested to shower blows upon the poor man instead of coming to his help in this terrible situation. Next he takes to task the educated of our country. "So long as the millions live in hunger and ignorance I hold every man a traitor who, having been educated at their expense, pays not the least heed to them', said Vivekananda. He regarded the neglect of the masses as a great national sin.

Vivekananda was fully convinced that only through education the lot of the poor can be improved here. Through education we should develop in them their lost individuality, once they become conscious of their human dignity, they would naturally try to rise up from their miserable state. But he was very much disappointed to see that nothing substantial has been done for educating the people. The germs of spirituality stored in our sacred books have to be brought to the common man. This can be done by spreading education among the masses through the medium of mother tongue. Ideas can easily be understood and assimilated even by the common-eat man if they are taught through their own mother-tongue. Our duty is to give those ideas and culture. "Without giving them culture, there can be no permanence in the raised condition of the masses", Vivekananda warned. Besides, they must be instructed in simple words about the necessities of -life and in trade, commerce, agriculture etc.

Once the poor man is made conscious of his strength, that he is the 'Omnipotent' and the 'Omniscient', the rest of the work becomes easy. The moment a fisherman thinks that he is spirit; he will be a better fisherman. Likewise a student becomes a better student, too. But so long as the novelty of the people is not banished, the hope of mass education remains a pious wish. For, even if free schools are opened in villages, the children would rather so to help their parents in their work or try to make a living than going to the school, if the poor bony cannot come to school for education, education must go to him.

Spiritual Development through Education

There are different types of education for spiritual development viz., Religious Education, Yoga Education, Moral Education…etc.

Religious Education – Spiritual Development

Hinduism is the world's oldest religious tradition; it goes back to the very dawn of history. The hymns composed some 5,000 years ago are still recited today.

Hinduism is the third largest of the world's religions, after Christianity and Islam. Nearly one-seventh of humanity calls Hinduism their spiritual home. Millions more in South and Southeast Asia and in the Far East trace their spiritual roots to Hinduism.

Hinduism is also the world's largest pluralistic tradition. A multiplicity of spiritual paths and ways are recognized as valid in Hinduism. Hinduism is not based on the teachings of a single Prophet or a single Book. The teachings of many different sages and saints find home within Hinduism. God may be worshiped both in male and female forms. Hinduism has much in common with the earth based religious traditions of the world.

Hinduism is not a creedal religion, based on dogma. Its emphasis is not on correct belief but on search for the Truth. The scripture describes several paths to spiritual development. The mountain peak may be reached by taking any of the several paths.

Sri Aurobindo (1872-1950), the great Indian seer of the first half of the twentieth century declared that Hinduism (also known as *Sanatan Dharma* or the eternal tradition) was rising not for India alone but for the world. Arnold Toynbee in his *A Study of History* was of the view that Hinduism will gain the status of a world religion in the new century.

Hindus believe that Reality is One – Ekam Sat. This Reality is everywhere, in everything, in every being. It is one and many at the same time and it also transcends them both. At the popular level, the One Reality is worshipped as the Trinity: Brahma the creator, Vishnu the preserver and Shiva the dissolver. Brahma, Vishnu and Shiva are not different gods, but they represent different faces of the One Supreme. Brahma, Vishnu and Shiva have their respective female consorts: Saraswati, Lakshmi and Durga. Even though God is One, Hindus worship God in a number of both male and female forms. Ram Swarup puts the matter this way:

Spiritual life is one but it is vast and rich in expression. The human mind conceives it differently. If the human mind was uniform without different depths, heights and levels of subtlety; or if all men had the same mind, the same psyche, the same imagination, the same needs, in short, if all men were the same, then perhaps One God would do. But a man's mind is not a fixed quantity and men and their powers and needs are different. So only some form of polytheism alone can do justice to this variety and richness.

— The Word As Revelation: Names of Gods, 1980.

FOUR PATHS: Hinduism prescribes four ways of spiritual salvation, depending on the personality of the seeker.

1. For the active person, there is Karma yoga, the path of selfless works.
2. For the contemplative and intellectual person, there is Jnana Yoga, the path of Knowledge.
3. For the emotional person, there is Bhakti yoga, the path of love and surrender. Bhakti yoga is said to be similar to the Christian path of love.
4. Finally, Raja yoga is the path of meditative exercises including concentration and one-pointedness. This path focusing on meditation has become popular in the West

Yoga Education – Spiritual Development

The Eight Limbs (Ashtanga) of Raja Yoga

The eight "limbs" or steps prescribed in the second *pada* of the Yoga Sutras are: *Yama, Niyama, Asana, Pranayama, Pratyahara, Dharana, Dhyana* and *Samadhi.*

Ashtanga yoga consists of the following steps: The first five are called external aids to Yoga (bahiranga sadhana)

- ❑ **Yama** refers to the five abstentions. These are the same as the five vows of Jainism.
  - **Ahimsa**: non-violence, inflicting no injury or harm to others or even to one's ownself, it goes as far as nonviolence in thought, word and deed.
  - **Satya**: truth in word & thought.
  - **Asteya**: non-covetousness, to the extent that one should not even desire something that is not his own.
  - **Brahmacharya**: abstain from sexual intercourse; celibacy in case of unmarried people and monogamy in case of married people. Even this to the extent that one should not possess any sexual thoughts towards any other man or woman except one's own spouse. It's common to associate Brahmacharya with celibacy.
  - **Aparigraha**: non-possessiveness
- ❑ **Niyama** refers to the five observances
  - **Shaucha**: cleanliness of body & mind.
  - **Santosha**: satisfaction; satisfied with what one has.
  - **Tapas**: austerity and associated observances for body discipline & thereby mental control.
  - **Svadhyaya**: study of the Vedic scriptures to know about God and the soul, which leads to introspection on a greater awakening to the soul and God within,
  - **Ishvarapranidhana**: surrender to (or worship of) God.

- **Asana**: Discipline of the body: rules and postures to keep it disease-free and for preserving vital energy. Correct postures are a physical aid to meditation, for they control the limbs and nervous system and prevent them from producing disturbances.
- **Pranayama**: control of breath. Beneficial to health, steadies the body and is highly conducive to the concentration of the mind.
- **Pratyahara**: withdrawal of senses from their external objects.

The last three levels are called internal aids to Yoga (antaranga sadhana)

- **Dharana**: concentration of the citta upon a physical object, such as a flame of a lamp, the mid point of the eyebrows, or the image of a deity.
- **Dhyana**: steadfast meditation. Undisturbed flow of thought around the object of meditation (pratyayaikatanata). The act of meditation and the object of meditation remain distinct and separate.
- **Samadhi**: oneness with the object of meditation. There is no distinction between act of meditation and the object of meditation. Samadhi is of two kinds:

Samprajnata Samadhi conscious samadhi. The mind remains concentrated (ekagra) on the object of meditation, therefore the consciousness of the object of meditation persists. Mental modifications arise only in respect of this object of meditation.

This state is of four kinds:

- Savitarka: the Citta is concentrated upon a gross object of meditation such as a flame of a lamp, the tip of the nose, or the image of a deity.
- Savichara: the Citta is concentrated upon a subtle object of meditation , such as the tanmatras
- Sananda: the Citta is concentrated upon a still subtler object of meditation, like the senses.

- Sasmita: the Citta is concentrated upon the ego-substance with which the self is generally identified.

Asamprajnata Samadhi supraconscious. The citta and the object of meditation are fused together. The consciousness of the object of meditation is transcended. All mental modifications are checked (niruddha), although latent impressions may continue.

Combined simultaneous practice of Dhâranâ, Dhyâna & Samâdhi is referred to as Samyama and is considered a tool of achieving various perfections, or Siddhis.

Yoga and Religion

Yoga is not a religion. It has no creed or fixed set of beliefs, nor is there a prescribed godlike figure to be worshipped in a particular manner. Religions for the most part seem to be based upon the belief in and worship of things (God or godlike figures) that exist outside one-self. The core of Yoga's philosophy is that everything is supplied from within the individual. Thus, there is no dependence on an external figure, either in the sense of a person or god figure, or a religious organization.

The common belief that Yoga derives from Hinduism is a misconception. Yoga actually predates Hinduism by many centuries. Ancient seals unearthed in the Indus Valley provide clear evidence of widespread Yoga practice earlier than 3,000 B.C.E. The techniques of Yoga have been adopted by Hinduism as well as by other world religions. Yoga is a system of techniques that can be used for a number of goals, from simply managing stress better, learning to relax, and increasing limberness all the way to becoming more self-aware and acquiring the deepest knowledge of one's own self.

The practice of Yoga will not interfere with any religion. Many American Yoga Association students who have practiced Yoga intensively for many years continue to follow the religious traditions they have grown up in or adopted without conflict.

Swami Vivekananda Spiritual Quotes

1. Anything that brings spiritual, mental or physical weakness, touch it not with the toes of your feet.
2. Be brave! Be strong! Be fearless! Once you have taken up the spiritual life, fight as long as there is any life in you. Even though you know you are going to be killed, fight till you "are killed." Don't die of fright. Die fighting. Don't go down till you are knocked down.
3. BY the study of different RELIGIONS we find that in essence they are one.
4. By the Vedas no books are meant. They mean the accumulated treasury of spiritual laws discovered by different persons in different times. Just as the law of gravitation existed before its discovery, and would exist if all humanity forgot it, so is it with the laws that govern the spiritual world
5. External nature is only internal nature writ large.
6. Give up all desire for enjoyment in earth or heaven. Control the organs of the senses and control the mind. Bear every misery without even knowing that you are miserable. Think of nothing but spiritual freedom.
7. GOD is to be worshipped as the one beloved, dearer than everything in this and next life.
8. God is very merciful to those whom He sees struggling heart and soul for spiritual realization. But remain idle, without any struggle, and you will see that His grace will never come.
9. GOD of truth, be Thou alone my guide...
10. Let us put forth all our energies to acquire that which never fails—our spiritual perfection. If we have true yearning for realization, we must struggle, and through struggle growth will come. We shall make mistakes, but they may be angels unawares.
11. Never think there is anything impossible for the soul. It is the greatest heresy to think so. If there is sin, this is the only sin? To say that you are weak, or others are weak.

12. Our supreme duty is to advance toward freedom—physical, mental, and spiritual—and help others to do so.
13. Records of great spiritual men of the past do us no good whatever except that they urge us onward to do the same, to experience religion ourselves.
14. Renunciation is the background of all religious thought wherever it be, and you will always find that as this idea of renunciation lessens, the more will the senses creep into the field of religion, and spirituality will decrease in the same ratio.
15. Salvation is not achieved by inactivity but by spiritual activities.
16. Save the spiritual store in your body by observing continence.
17. "Seek ye first the kingdom of God, and everything shall be added unto you".This is the one great duty, this is renunciation. Live for an ideal, and leave no place in the mind for anything else. Let us put forth all our energies to acquire that which never fails—our spiritual perfection. If we have true yearning for realization, we must struggle, and through struggle growth will come. We shall make mistakes, but they may be angels unawares.
18. Take up one idea. Make that one idea your life - think of it, dream of it, live on that idea. Let the brain, muscles, nerves, every part of your body, be full of that idea, and just leave every other idea alone. This is the way to success that is way great spiritual giants are produced.
19. The animal has its happiness in the senses, the human beings in their intellect, and the gods in spiritual contemplation. It is only to the soul that has attained to this contemplative state that the world really becomes beautiful.
20. The first sign of your becoming religious is that you are becoming cheerful
21. The greatest help to spiritual life is meditation. In meditation we divest ourselves of all material conditions and feel our divine nature. We do not depend upon any external help in meditation. The touch of the soul can paint the brightest color even in the dingiest places; it can cast a fragrance over the vilest thing; it

can make the wicked divine—and all enmity, all selfishness is effaced.

22. The more we come out and do good to others, the more our hearts will be purified, and God will be in them.
23. This is the great lesson that we are here to learn through myriads of births and heavens and hells—that there is nothing to be asked for, desired for, beyond one's spiritual Self (atman).
24. Tremendous purity, tremendous renunciation, is the one secret of spirituality. "Neither through wealth, nor through progeny, but through renunciation alone is immortality to be reached," say the Vedas. "Sell all that thou hast and give to poor, and follow me," says the Christ. So all great saints and prophets have expressed it, and have carried it out in their lives. How can great spirituality come without renunciation?
25. We are what our thoughts have made us; so take care about what you think. Words are secondary. Thoughts live; they travel far.
26. What is material and what is not material? When the world is the end and God the means to attain that end, then that is material. When God is the end and the world is only the means to attain that end, spirituality has begun.
27. Where can we go to find God if we cannot see Him in our own hearts and in every living being.
28. You cannot believe in God until you believe in yourself.
29. You have to grow from the inside out. None can teach you, none can make you spiritual. There is no other teacher but your own soul.

Conclusions

Inculcation of Spiritual values in each and every student is important. Today we are facing so many problems like terrorism, poverty, corruption, illiteracy, alcoholism and teenage pregnancy. Terrorism is the most dangerous problem in the modern world. The only cause for all these problems is lack of spiritual knowledge. We are giving priority or importance for external world. "*Brahma Satyam, Jagat Mithya, and Jivo Brahmaiva naparah*"... according this the ultimate reality is Brahman. There is no difference between self and Brahman. If any one loves God, definitely he loves fellow human beings. Love and affection towards fellow human beings, animals and plants is more important. Spiritual knowledge gives discriminative power- what is right? What is wrong? Which is good? Which is bad? What is right way? Etc. It is the duty of parents and teacher to develop spiritual values in the students. Education is power. Through Education it is easy to inculcate spiritual knowledge in the students. According to swami Vivekananda education means that character is formed, strength of mind is increased, and intellect is sharpened, as a result of which one can stand on one's own feet. It is the fore most duty of government to provide such type of education for all.

References

1. Amareswaran, N. (2010). "*Moral Values of Intermediate Students*", Discovery Publication, New Delhi.
2. Amareswaran, N. (2011): "*Importance of Yoga for Human Wellbeing*", edited by Anjana Kaul, Discovery Publication, New Delhi.
3. Goel, Madan Lal. "*Religious Tolerance and Hinduism*", unpublished article.
4. Sudipa Dutta Roy (2001). "*Education in the Vision of Swami Vivekananda*", published in 'e-Samskriti: The Essence of Indian Culture', online article.

CHAPTER–7

Realizing Self through Aesthetic Experience

Dr. Arti Srivastava,
Army Institute of Education,
Delhi

Enjoying the rhythmic nature of the universe by using different styles of expressions in the form of poetry, painting, singing or any other medium defines individual as an aesthetic being. Aesthetics is the study of value in the realm of value. It is a fruitful way of exploring one's personal being, of entering upon the journey of self-discovery. It facilitates us to actualize the essence of the self, and, particularly, to feelings and emotions. It helps us to discover the sensitivity which opens those dimensions of reality that lie beyond mental constructs.

The experience of listening to a music, reciting a poetry or painting scenes in nature is distinctive, emotional and contemplative in character. We experience these things in a special vocabulary which is beautiful, exquisite, inspiring and moving experience. This can be characterized as aesthetic experience. Tagore's philosophy of 'Anandyoga' emphasizes aesthetic experiences as an important aspect for developing a harmonious personality where creative self is realized through aesthetic experiences in harmony with the universal self. According to him man through the process of creative self expression extends himself at different levels as physical man, personal man, artistic man, religious man, universal and spiritual man. Tagore's aesthetic approach is about achieving growth in consciousness. Principle of harmony is the main idea of Tagore's thought which is manifested in art and literature. The aesthetic sense Rasa is also operative in the process of integration. He perceives man evolving from the lower forms of life to its highest expression. The tradition of Indian aesthetic in its classical form speaks about the essence of feeling ['Rasanubhuti'] which is an integral part of human existence. This is related to finer sensitivities of life. The process of sensitization starts in the beginning when the mother looks at the child. The communication of feeling of pleasure through different gestures and expressions is termed as 'Vatsalya rasa' . There isn't any parameter to define and measure this feeling. Artists and poets have tried to express this feeling beautifully through paintings and poems but aesthetic feeling is the matter of individual sensitivity. The concept of 'Rasa' the aesthetic cognition according to is founded upon the verity of feeling which has less to do with the concept of universal in its logical sense. Rasa is both the essence of feeling and what is tasted or aesthetically enjoyed. According to Sri Aurobindo :

"The different faces of life are meant to be expressed and manifested by the Ananda. Love and Beauty are powers of Ananda as Light and Knowledge are of Consciousness"[1].

'The connection between Beauty, Rasa and Ananda can hardly be realized except by experience of Ananda. Ananda is not an ordinary mental state. Rasa is the mind's understanding of beauty and pleasure in it accompanied usually by the vital's enjoyment of it [Bhoga]. Mental pleasure is not Ananda, but only derivations from the concealed universal Ananda of the Spirit in things.'[2]

Gadamer believed that it is not aesthetic consciousness, but the experience of art or art experience which is more important...

"the work of art is not an object that stands over against a subject for itself. Instead the work of art has its true being in the fact that it becomes an experience changing the person experiencing it."[3]

The aesthetic feeling as a finer sensitivity of human existence provides scope for creation and appreciation. Aesthetics as a way of life defines an individual as a creative being who connects himself with the world in a manner so that all the creative forces work in harmony. Aesthetics, or creativity is not without effort or preparation, it results from a dialogue with one's inner being and with the larger Self which provides us with freedom, life and the potential for maturation..

Aesthetics also has to do with appreciation. Not only are we capable of producing beautiful things, we are also sensitive to appreciate the expressions of others. What they produce may enhance what we contribute to the general good Aesthetics as the creation and appreciation of beauty finds expression in number of ways which includes drawing, painting, sculpture, architecture, music, writing, prose or poetry, dance, computer images, films, and supremely in the living of one's life. The ability to respond aesthetically and the opportunity to appreciate art are important component of a well being and this is reflected in the choices we make for our life. The choices that we make daily in designing our enviourment manifest aesthetic preferences. A human being can not be called fully developed until and unless he has this capacity of responding aesthetically.

The distinctive feature of aesthetic expression is that it has to be free from desire and detached from any personal involvement.

'That is the right consciousness ,not to desire or to be attached to the possession of anything for oneself ,but to take the universal beauty etc. for a spiritual selfless Ananda'.[4]

Appreciation of an art form demands judgments which is individualistic in nature. This capacity helps him to evolve as a sensitive being. Aesthetic judgments is regarded as exemplifying taste by Hume and Kant because aesthetic judgments on an object requires personal acquaintance and a felt response to an object is a necessary condition for this. Secondly there is not any rule and principle which can be termed as aesthetic properties.

Judging according to rules is actually missing the uniqueness of objects and thus failing to judge aesthetically. Aesthetic subjectivism denies that aesthetic qualities inhere in objects, and maintains that in aesthetic experience I am affected by the object and my response does not consist in knowledge of it's properties but pleasure is considered as essential to the experience which grounds an aesthetic judgments according to Kant[1987].Kant was the first to give a clear and convincing argument for the autonomy of art, he owed the autonomy of art to human subjectivity which is capable of achieving a psychical distance as a factor of art and aesthetic principle. Art is independent of its empirical reasons.

Aesthetics-"that whose determining ground can be no other than subjective".[5]

Aesthetic object is a subjective existence. The universality of an aesthetic judgment is subjective.

Kant combines sense intuition and contemplative mode of thinking. He confirms that aesthetic consciousness is experiential in character and aesthetic cognition can not be completely cut off from other perspectives of freedom.

'Every aesthetic production starts from an essentially infinite separation of the activities which are separated in all free productions. But as these activities are to be represented in the product as in union, this product represents an infinite in finite form. The infinite represented in finite form is beauty.[6]

Aesthetics provides an opportunity to touch the infinite reality within us and enables us to realize the peace which is in inner harmony, Inner harmony dwells in truth and not in any outer adjustment. This facilitates an individual to integrate the sensory experience with the inner self and appreciate. 'Beauty carries an eternal assurance of our spiritual relationship to reality which waits for its perfection in the response of our love." This is the reason that whenever we create something we try to put our soul in it and while looking at the creation we always find our image into it. The subject of enjoyment unconsciously affects and is affected by the object. The object is not just a factual appearance but it has inherent value attached to it. which is an enjoyable look or expression The subject doesn't feel detached from the object ,he feels attracted into or weighed down by the object. This relationship can be understood as an aesthetic dialogue where the artist and the creation interact and develop senstivity for each other which help them to discover their creative self .

Appreciation of art provides most complex and intense form of aesthetic experience.

"Art reveals man's wealth of life, which seeks it's freedom in forms of perfection which are an end in themselves".[7]

For Tagore aesthetics expression is joyous meeting and union with the 'Real outside him'. He believes that it's through relationship we understand the world outside which enables him to realize his self.

"Reality is not based in the substance of things but in the principle of relationship".[8]

Tagore perceives unity in the different art forms[this is the reason that a beautiful composition in any language gives immense joy and pleasure] and this can be characterized by the rhythm of a poem, a beautiful picture, a song, a character or a harmony of inter related ideas or facts. The creation as an expression of the varied forms of self realization manifests the creativity of life.

Tagore's man is an artist who has the capacity to respond creatively. According to him man creatively perceives, integrates and transforms relational life. Creativity is the conscious expression of the personality. For Tagore personality is.........."a self conscious principle of living unity, it at once comprehends and yet transcends all the detail of facts that are individually mine, my knowledge, feelings, wish and will, my memory, my hope my love, my activities and all my belongings."[9]

This suggests that the man finds his ways of expressing creatively, Art as a creation of human personality unfolds individual's relationship to reality.

"Personality discloses relationships and creatively expresses this reality in art when one functions on a higher level of consciousness. Because Principle of 'uninterrupted relation' is the structure of personality on this level of consciousness, art becomes an expression of personality itself."[10]

For Tagore within the process of perception and integration man functions as an artist because all his sensitivities -sympathy, participation, joy and love- integrate him in his relationships. The experience of relationships bring a change and transformation to life. Transformation for Tagore is an element of human growth which is the part of artistic process itself. Creativity and life are connected. The pursuit of art for him is the pursuit of life. Tagore found art and life forming an integral whole 'Because art emerges from the deepest experience of man and reflects the highest expression of life'.[11]

Tagore's aesthetics is integrated with religion also. Religion according to him is the expression of whole man and not limited to one dimension of man. The religious man draws upon all human sensitivity in order to experience the divine in humanity, he enters with feelings, emotion and passion into the finite world. The personality of religious man is fulfilled in the same manner as are other levels of life, namely in relationships. man's relationship with finite and infinite raises him in his conscious experience of reality. Religious consciousness for Tagore is achieved in the love relationship between parmatman (universal self) and the jivatman (individual self).

Man with these sensitivities of being artistic, religious and continually evolving with the relational experiences gets connected to the reality as creative and the divine as Creator. Gradually by becoming conscious of the inter-relationships of the created order man approaches the divine principle of unity that constitutes the interrelationship of things. " Creation is the expression of the Creator –Artist, the Infinite Personality, who seeks continual self expression. The divine who is similar to man ,stands incomplete and unfulfilled unless he fins expression. The personality of the divine is fulfilled as is the personality of the man: in the growth of relationships. As the Creator –Artist expresses himself in creation, his relationships are extended and the divine principle of unity is manifested in created order."[12]

Man by nature is an artist and it is an art kingdom, which with it's endless panorama of beautiful shapes completes him by bringing him to an experience of the wholeness of life. Thus art becomes an expression of personality itself. Aesthetic expression in the form of appreciation and creation can find outlet with the conscious effort of education. Thus aesthetics is a fruitful way of exploring one's personal being, of entering upon the journey of self-discovery A learner can continually exercise joy and freedom and at the same time evaluate and evolve in order to have best of education. Therefore process of education should be living and pulsating so that the learners are stimulated to have a natural and spontaneous experience with joy and freedom.

Foot Notes

1) Sri Aurobindo -Letters on Poetry, Literature and Art
2) Sri Aurobindo-Letters on Poetry, Literature and Art
3) Hans- George Gadamer: Truth and Method, The Seabury Press, New York 1975, p92
4) Sri Aurobindo Letters on Poetry, Literature and Art
5) Immanual Kant, Critique of Judgment, trans. By J.H. Bernard, Hafner publishing co. New York and London.1968 P.37

6) Bernard Bosanquet: A history of Aesthetics, George Allen & Unwin Ltd, London,1966, p.319
7) R.Tagore, The Religion Of An Artist
8) Religion of Man, p.84
9) Tagore, "The religion of an Artist" Contemporary Indian Philosophy, ed. S. Radhakrishnan & J.H. Muirhead [NewYork Mcmillan Company 1936
10) Tagore- sadhana
11) William Cenkner 'The Hindu Personality in Education'.
12) William Cenkner 'The Hindu Personality

References

Tagore,R. "The Religion Of Man", Visva Bharti Publishing Calcutta

Tagore,R. "The Religion Of An Artist" Visva Bharati Calcutta

Biswas Goutam, "Art as Dialogue" Essays in Phenomenology of Aesthetic Experience, Indira Gandhi National Centre for Art and Culture, DK Print world N. Delhi 1995

Blackwell Companion To Philosophy, edition II.

Cenkner, William,"The Hindu Personality In Education, Manohar 1976

Sri Aurobindo, 'Letters on Poetry, Literature and Art, Sri Aurobindo Ashram,Pondicherry.

Journal of Indian Council of Philosophical Research , Vol xxiv number 4, 2007

CHAPTER–8

EDUCATION FOR SPIRITUAL DEVELOPMENT IN SCHOOL STUDENTS

Dr. G.K. Joneja,
Associate Professor,
NCERT, New Delhi

Past decade/turn of century have seen economic developments and materialistic abundance which has resulted into materialistic approach to life devoid of spiritual, moral and human values. This is a life in which not only an individual but the society as a whole has plunged into deep crisis. The crisis is reflected in the ever growing needs (or say greeds); insatiable desires; unrealistic ambitions; false ego; exhibition of wealth and might; self-centeredness; unhappiness and dissatisfaction with life; aggression; violence; crime; lawlessness; corruption; stress; depression; suicides; breaking of families etc. No one can stop or need to stop economic developments and monetary gains. However, in such situation, individuals can be prepared to lead a balanced life by filling gap between materialism and humanism which is possible through holistic development of their personalities i.e. intellectual, social, emotional, aesthetic, moral and spiritual. Only human beings are endowed with both material nature and spiritual nature and have potential to develop spiritual qualities. In fact they have both materialistic and spiritual requirements.

Spiritual development, well being and quality of life

Generally, the focus on the name of overall development of personality of students in schools remains on development of intellectual, personal-social and emotional aspects of life and spiritual development is neglected. May be that spirituality is traditionally thought in relation to religion or equated with religion and not beyond it. Therefore, it could not be integrated into the formal education system.

Researches have differentiated between religion and spirituality, with one distinction being that religion generally implies involvement with specific rituals and faith communities (Emmons and Paloutzian, 2003), whereas spirituality refers to more individual pursuits of the sacred and may not take place within a religions context (Steger & Frazier, 2005). However, religion is one of the ways through which spiritual development takes place. The spiritual aspect of religion or spiritualism contains wisdom which enables one to transform one's quality of life to live to the full fruitfully and meaningfully (Dhokalia 2001).

Spiritual development is a process of growth of inner self leading to comprehensive self development which is reflected in finding purpose and meaning of life as well as its connectedness to the humanity.

Spiritually developed persons personify all-round development. Besides physical and intellectual development, they are equipped with eternal human values like social and ethical values which widen their vision and understanding of human life as a journey towards higher ideals. One major quality is that these people have a sense of meaning and purpose of life. They are understanding, tolerant, open-minded, peaceful, truthful, honest, just, courageous, compassionate, practice universal love, service and purity, dedicated, shun ritualism, devoid of superstition, have scientific temperament / thought, philosophical thinking, devotion to duty without expectations, self-analytical ability etc. They personify wisdom and are source of inspiration to others. Above all they have spiritual quest to attain the highest level of consciousness.

Spirituality and spiritual experiences are positively associated with well-being (Mac Donald, 2000). The quality of human life has largely depended on man's cultivation of goodness and spiritual and enlightened perspective (Dhokalia, 2001). Maulana Wahiduddin Khan (2002) believes in intellectual awakening as intellectuals and wise men make the nation. Considerable psychological research has demonstrated that spirituality and religiousness are positively co-related to a variety of life situations including but not limited to, illness recovery, ability to cope with stress, disease occurrence, morality, self-esteem, and overall satisfaction with life. (Miller & Thoresen, 2003; Powell, Shahabi, & Thoresen, 2003). Duffy and Blustein (2005) found that religiousness and spirituality play a significant role in an individual's career development. Many a times our counsellors use students' spirituality in personal-social and career counselling. Teachers, counsellors and helping professionals need to be spiritually developed persons. Everts (2003) reported that peer counsellors preferred have sense of the meaning and purpose of life. They have positive attitude towards people, problems, challenging situations and understand themselves and others at a psychological level.

During recent decades, spiritual development has drawn a lot of attention from all quarts – educationists, psychologists, scholars, policy makers and society in general. Spiritual growth, spiritual values, spiritual awakening, spiritual enlightenment. heightened consciousness; intellectual awakening, spiritual intelligence or SQ etc. are used to refer to spiritual development. Even terms like cosmic intelligence, soul's intelligence, self-actualization etc. are also found in literature on this subject.

Spiritual Intelligence (SI) or Spiritual Quotient (SQ) are relatively new terms. Spiritual Intelligence measured as Spiritual

Quotient (SQ) is the intelligence with which persons address and solve problems of meaning and other higher values of life. It is our ultimate intelligence as Zohar and Marshall (2001) says "Neither IQ or EQ separately or in combination is enough to explain the full complexity of human intelligence". SQ is the foundation for balanced use of IQ and EQ. Zohar and Marshall provide information on the brain's third neural system and the "God Spot" which appears to be placed in all human beings and basis for spiritual development. They introduced the following 12 qualities of SQ:

- ❑ Self-awareness: Knowing what I believe in and value, and what deeply motivates me
- ❑ Spontaneity: Living in and being responsive to the moment
- ❑ Being vision – and value – led : Acting from principles and deep beliefs, and living accordingly
- ❑ Holism : Seeing larger patterns, relationships, and connections; having a sense of belonging
- ❑ Compassion : having the quality of "feeling-with" and deep empathy
- ❑ Celebration of diversity : Valuing other people for their differences, not despite them
- ❑ Field independence: Standing against the crowd and having one's own convictions
- ❑ Humility : Having the sense of being a player in a larger drama, of one's true place in the world
- ❑ Tendency to ask fundamental "Why?" questions: Needing to understand things and get to the bottom of them
- ❑ Ability to reframe: standing back from a situation or problem and seeing the bigger picture; seeing problems in a wider context
- ❑ Positive use of adversity : Learning and growing from mistakes, setbacks, and suffering
- ❑ Sense of vocation: Feeling called upon to serve, to give something back

The spiritual intelligence offers a new perspective and way to bring together the cognitive, emotional and spiritual intelligence along with the material concepts of present time to formulate a vision, which is in fact a new reality (Nagpal & Joneja, 2005).

Spiritual development vs. development of spiritual values

Traditionally, spiritual development is considered as a part of development of values and taken care under value development programmes. The Eighty first report on value based education (Rajya Sabha, Parliament of India, Jan 1999) has mentioned five core universal values, namely, truth, righteous conduct, peace, love and non-violence on which the value based education programme can be built up. The five universal values are linked with five domains of human personality - intellectual, physical, emotional, psychological and spiritual which are correspondingly correlated with five major objectives of education, namely, knowledge, skills, balance, vision and identity, Sathya Sai organization's programme for value education is based on the above mentioned five universal values.

Like other areas of human development, the process of spiritual development also begins very early as children start imbibing values at a tender age in the home atmosphere. The school stage is the most impressionable stage of development. The importance of school years and expectations from the schools for inculcation of human values among students led many institutions to plan programme for value development.

Joshi (2003) discussed three important foundations (grounds) on which value-oriented education can be established:

i. Widening of Consciousness : Values through Astronomy, Geography and Mathematics

ii. Deepening of consciousness : Values through Languages, Poetry and Art.

iii. Heightening of Consciousness : Values through methods of demonstration, dramas and exhibitions.

The schools engaged in seriously educating students for the Fundamental Duties of Citizens contribute to students' spiritual development. Though the duties make our citizens good human beings, some of the duties such as to promote harmony and spirit of common brotherhood; to value and preserve the rich heritage of our composite culture; to protect and improve natural environment and have compassion for living creatures; to develop the scientific temper, humanism and the spirit of inquiry and reform; to safeguard public property and adjure violence; to strive towards excellence in all spheres of individual and collective activity have direct bearing on students' developing spiritual qualities.

About 5000 institutions belonging to various sects / communities / societies impart value education of which education for spiritual development is a part. The research studies on effectiveness of value education programmes and approaches followed by various institutions are limited. The countable studies include Pinkeerani (1981), Sarangi (1994), Nanda (1997), Bagchi (2001), Joneja (2002). Among these, only Nanda's (1997) sociological study of value education approaches of 12 schools of different religious sects and missions draws conclusions on worthiness functional and universal application aspects of different approaches. May be in near future, many more studies of conclusive nature can suggest effective approaches for development of human values and more particularly spiritual development.

All the schools even if they don't follow a particular approach or philosophy or structured programme try to inculcate values and promote spiritual development through a variety of activities, practices, experiences in their own way. All the school experiences have potential for spiritual development of students. In a study of value based practices of privately managed schools, Joneja (2002) found that most of the school practices including teaching of subjects, prayer, assembly, yoga, meditation, literary activities, fine arts, sports, games, music, dance, drama, quizzes, clubs, celebrations of national international days or anniversaries; of great personalities, school magazine, social service programmes, projects, interaction with eminent persons, visits/ tours etc. had great potential for development of human values.

There was overlap of values developed through different activities. However, these values represent the qualities of spiritually developed persons. The main values emerged included : Oneness of humanity, citizenship, equality, integrity, humanism, inner peace, kindness, compassion, caring, sharing, honesty and truthfulness, humbleness, fearless, self-control, self-confidence, consciousness, happiness, curiosity, observation, creativity, objectivity, openness, appreciation, critical thinking, logical reasoning, quest for knowledge, discipline, dedication to work, team spirit, leadership, respect for different cultures and religions, human rights, respect for women and elders, social responsibility, social service, concern for environment etc. More specifically, students involvement in planning and implementation of activities; interaction with teachers and principal without inhibition and fear; no humiliation in the name of discipline; celebrations related to all regions, religions, cultures; social awareness and service programmes, community work had great impact on value development in students. The most important aspect was identification of objectives, inputs and the way learning experiences were organized for students that made a difference. In a NCERT project, four activities namely, story telling, street play, poster making and panel discussion were organized with the objective of development of values in students. The desired outcome available in the form of video programmes show the method of organization of the activities (Joneja, 2003).

Many teachers without formally naming or unconsciously are contributing to spiritual development of students by their conduct, example, during teaching-learning activities related to subject matter or other school experiences. Teachers already use various approaches and methods which promote values like positive thinking to reading, seeking and constructing knowledge, relating knowledge to different areas and people, developing creativity and critical thinking, open-mindedness, problem solving, decision making, truthfulness and objectivity; spirit of inquiry, appreciation for nature, respect for different cultures; social responsibility, non-violence etc. In fact the teacher's spiritual development and attitude and conviction is must in promoting the process of spiritual development.

A worth reporting experiment was done successfully in USA in 1947 which was published in the volume "Spiritual Values in the Elementary Schools – the Twenty – Sixth year Book" (1947) by the National Elementary Principal, a Bulletin of the Department of Elementary School Principals. In an article 'A Delayed Book Reading' on the above mentioned publication, Uppal (2001) narrated experiences from the reports presented by the Principals in 1947, based on their achievements, which emerge from initiatives taken by them collectively and carried out through cooperation of everyone in the schools. Such experiments from our schools if reported would be welcomed.

References

Bagchi, J.P. (2001). A study of school practices in value based education at primary level. Rajasthan : Regional Institute of Education (NCERT) Ajmer. (Mimeographed).

Dhokalia, R.P. (2001) Eternal human values and world religions. New Delhi: National Council of Educational Research and Training.

Duffy, R.D., & Blustein, D.L. (2005). The relationship between spirituality, religiousness and career adaptability. Journal of Vocational Behaviour, 67, 429-440.

Emmons, R.A., & Paloutzian, R.F. (2003). The psychology of religion. Annual Review of Psychology, 54, 377-402.

Everts, H. (2003). Peer counselling and support. In Garry hornby, Caroll Hall & Eric Hall (eds) Counselling pupils in schools : Skills and strategies for teachers. London : Routledge Falmer. (p.69-79).

Joneja, G.K. (2002). A study of value based practices in some selected schools. New Delhi : NCERT (mimeographed).

Joneja, G.K. (2003). Formulation of prototype programmes and guidelines for development of values. New Delhi : NCERT (mimeographed).

Joshi, K. (2003). Value education in schools: Strategies and Implementation. In J.S. Rajput (ed.). Value Education in Indian Schools : Experiences and Strategies of Implementation. New Delhi : NCERT (26-39).

Khan, M.W. (2002). Value orientation : Need for awakening. In J.S. Rajput (ed.). Value Education in Indian Schools : Experiences and Strategies of Implementation. New Delhi : NCERT (p.19-22).

MacDonald, D.A. (2000). Spirituality : Description, measurement, and relation to five factor model of personality. Journal of Personality, 68, 153-197.

Miller, W.R., & Thoresen, C.E. (2003). Spirituality, religion, and health : An emerging research field. American Psychologist, 58, 24-35.

Nagpal, S., & Joneja, G.K. (2005). Conceptual evolution of IQ, EQ and SQ. Perspectives in Education, 21 (4), 211-215.

Nanda, R.T. (1997). Contemporary approaches to value education in India. New Delhi : Regency Publication.

Pinkeerani (1981). Behaviour of students in and out of schools as related to their moral education – A study for curriculum change. Unpublished Ph.D. (Education) thesis. Chandigarh : Punjab University.

Powell, L.H., Shahabi, L., & Thoresen, C.E. (2003). Religion and spirituality : Linkages to physical health. American Psychologist, 58, 36-52.

Sarangi, R. (1994). Moral education in schools : Bases and implications. New Delhi : Deep and Deep Publications.

Steger, M.F., & Frazier, P. (2005). Meaning in Life : One link in the chain from religiousness to well-being. Journal of Counselling Psychology, 52 (4), 574-582.

Uppal, S. (July 2001). A delayed book reading 'Spiritual values in the elementary education'. Journal of Value Education, 1(2), 123-124.

Rajya Sabha, Parliament of India (1999). Department related parliamentary standing committee on human resource development : Eighty first report on value – based education. New Delhi : Rajya Sabha Secretariat (Mimeographed).

Zohar, D.K. & Marshall, I. (2000). SQ – Spiritual Intelligence – the ultimate Intelligence. London : Bloomsbury.

CHAPTER–9

Story Telling for Spiritual Education: Reflections of an ELT Practitioner

Pranita Gopal,
Asst Professor,
Army Institute of Education
Delhi Cantt., New Delhi

The genesis of this reflection

Serendipity is not limited to the discipline of the Sciences; our classrooms provide us with enough examples where we can acknowledge the benefit of a serendipitous moment. What began as an initiative to get my Pre-service B Ed English Language Teachers to read stories to improve their own reading, writing, speaking and listening skills in English; turned out to be an activity that brought together different aspects of education (per se) - very serendipitously within the Pre-service teacher education curricula.

A brief overview of this activity: As an ELT practitioner, I have always felt that majority of English Teachers aren't very fond of reading - anything. It is a very disappointing discovery that I make every year. Each year, I try something to encourage the pre-service to read beyond the prescribed texts and share what they read with the entire group - me included. This year, we had a storytelling session that lasted for a month; where every pre-service teacher had to come in front of the class and share a story. This story could be any story - inspirational devotional, personal anecdotes, love stories, classics, short stories- but the language of communication was to be English and was to last at least for five minutes.

The reflections presented here are painted on two broad canvases (which ultimately I hope to show as a continuum, seamlessly flowing into each other): one as an ELT practitioner; ELT learner and the second as a story-listener!

Presented below are two sample stories that were shared in the class. These stories were chosen as a part of this reflection for they help us delve deeper into the essence of spirituality and self- realisation.

Story 1: One day a young man was standing in the middle of the town, proclaiming that he had the most beautiful heart in the valley. A large crowd gathered and they all admired his heart because it was the perfect one. There was not even a single mark on it. Everybody in the crowd agreed that the young man was actually a man with the perfect heart! The young man began to boast about his beautiful heart in the valley, when an old man came to him and said, "Why do you think you have a beautiful and a perfect heart? Let me tell you, that it is not as perfect as mine!"

The young man and the crowd were shocked and surprised. They looked at the old man's heart. It was beating strongly, but it was full of scars. It had places where small pieces had been removed and other pieces put in but, the pieces didn't quite fit and there were some jagged edges. In fact in some places there were some deep gorges where whole pieces were missing.

The people starred at the old man and thought, "How could he say that his heart is more beautiful?" The young man looked at the old man's heart and started laughing. "You must be joking", said the young man. "Compare your heart with mine and mine is perfect and yours is a mess of scars and tears."

The old man said, "Yes, yours is perfect when you look at it, but I would never trade mine with yours. Every scar that you see represents a person to whom 1 have given my love, whenever I did that, I tore a piece of my heart and gave it to them. Often they gave me pieces of their own heart, which filled the empty spaces in my heart and because all the pieces are not exactly of the same size, I know there are rugged edges. I don't feel bad at all instead I cherish each piece as they remind me of the love I have shared. And sometimes, I have given pieces of my heart away and the other person hasn't returned apiece of his heart to me. These are those empty pieces, the empty gorges. " The old man continued, "Although these gorges are painful, they stay open and remind me of the love I have for these people, and I hope someday they may return and fill the empty gorges. So now do you see what true beauty is? "

The young man stood silently with tears running down his cheek. He went closer to the old man, and ripped a piece of his beautiful and young heart. He offered it to the . old man with trembling hands.

The old man took the offering, and placed it in his heart and then took a piece from his old scarred heart and placed it in the wound in the young man's heart. It fit, but, not perfectly and there were some rugged edges. The young man looked at his heart, not perfect anymore, but more beautiful than ever because the love from the old man's heart flowed into his.

Story 2: A group of frogs were travelling through the woods, when two of them fell into a deep pit. All the other frogs gathered around the pit. When they saw how deep it was, they told the two frogs that they were as good as dead. The two frogs ignored the comments and tried to jump up out of the pit with all of their might. The other frogs kept telling them to stop, that they were as good as dead. Finally, one of the frogs took heed to what the other frogs were saying and gave up. She fell down and died. The other frog continued to jump as hard as she could. Once again, the crowd of frogs yelled at her to stop the pain and just die. She began jumping even harder and finally made it out. When she got out, the other frogs said, "Did you not hear us?" The frog explained to them that she was deaf - she thought they were encouraging her to jump out of the hole the entire time.

Spiritual Education

We live in very interesting times, where there is an inverse ratio between the technological advancements and the quality of life. Although the world has turned into a global village, yet our neighbour remains distant. This lack of empathy between fellow human beings is reflected in our day to day conduct and the core value system that are an essential part of being human. The gap between what we are and what we should be, is so wide, that almost everyone experiences the void in various form and *essentially do not know what is to be done about it.* The void exerts its presence in the society by the regression of societal values and societal structure to the extent that today, most of us live in constant fear. It is here the role of Spiritual Education comes into play.

Spiritual Education is no different from other forms of education; instead it adds thrust to the entire process of education, learning, knowledge and knowing. Spiritual Education begins from the realm of knowing the surroundings and transcends into the dimensions of knowing thy self and in process knowing about the process of knowing and ultimately takes an individual to the realm of the limitless. It is about travelling from *here to there.* It might seem to be a tall order to realize this within the classroom, but then that is what education is. It is a tall order. It is about striving to be; to exist; to know and be known; and more essentially it about gathering the experiences that add meaning to the entire experience of being human.

Storytelling and Spiritual Education

Stories have always fascinated the human mind. All people have a basic need to share stories. Stories organize experiences and record important happenings. As common forms of discourse, stories are of great interest and significance in language and literacy development, especially when considering the increased linguistic and cultural diversity of students in the India classrooms. Stories enable teachers to learn about their students' cultures, experiences, and meaningful relationships. Through the sharing of stories, teachers and children "create the potential for new connections that link them together inside a new tale" (Dyson & Genishi, 1994).

Stories first arise in the context of relationships when small children acquire the ability to verbalize their experiences. With this verbalization, children become the "narrated selves" of their own lives, sharing interpretations with others. Like adults, children use narrative to shape and reshape their lives, imagining what could have or should have happened, and reviewing what actually did happen (Stern, 1985). Thus stories have interrelated social and evaluative functions (Dyson & Genishi, 1994). The stories we tell help define our socio-cultural landscape in particular ways and demonstrate connections between language, culture, and power (Dakhtin, 1981).

Storytelling is as old as mankind, predating any other form of oral history (Zabel, 1991). Joseph Campbell believes that stories in the form of myths represent "a cacophonous chorus" that began when our primal ancestors told stories about the animals they killed for food and the supernatural world to which they thought the animals departed after death. People tell stories in an attempt to come to terms with the world and harmonize their lives with reality (Flowers, 1988). Stories have been used since time immemorial to record important events, celebrate the feats of heroes and heroines, transmit the spirit and facts of a major occurrence, and point out patterns of human experience and behavior. Storytelling is a cornerstone of the teaching profession (Zabel, 1991).

Researchers have noted the significance of storytelling in oral cultures that have persisted over time. Stories help tribe members to make sense of their collective experiences, such as illness, death, and conflict, as well as interrelationships, including courtship, marriage, childbirth, and stewardship of nature. An oral culture teaches tribe members to preserve the wisdom of their heritage, transmit skills, maintain respect for elders, and understand how children fit into their lives (Van Groenou, 1995).

Stories are very powerful mediums that help the listener connect with what is being said. Table 1 lists famous genres of stories that are used in and for Spiritual Education.

Story Genres in and for Spiritual Education

1. **Panchatantra Stories:** In the Indian tradition, The Panchatantra is a nitisastra. Niti can be roughly translated as "the wise conduct of life". It draws from the Dharma and Arthasastras, quoting them extensively. The Panchatantra. is essentially connected with one of the branches of science known by the Indians as the 'Nitishastra' which in Sanskrit means 'A book of wise conduct in life'. It attempts to teach us, how to understand people, bow to choose reliable and trustworthy friends, how to meet difficulties and solve problems through tact and wisdom, and how to live in peace and harmony in the face of hypocrisy, deceit and many pitfalls in life. The Panchatantra is woven round the frame of a tale of a king who entrusts his three 'dud' sons to a learned man, a Brahmin, called Pandit Vishnu Sharma, to enlighten their minds within six months. The Brahmin promises to educate them and takes them to his 'ashrama' (hermitage). There he recites to them his specially composed tales divided into five tantras (in Sanskrit: Pancha=five and tantra=systems or parts) of how to deal with people in life. The language of the author is both artistic and elegant. The tale is narrated in prose while the exposition of a philosophical and moral theme is put in verse, maxims or wise sayings are also expressed in verse, which either sums up the narration or introduces the next tale.

2. **Jataka Tales**: These are the stories that tell about the previous lives of the Buddha, in both human and animal form. The future Buddha may appear in them as a king, an outcast, a god, an elephant-but, in whatever form, he exhibits some virtue that the tale thereby inculcates. Jataka Tales are apart of the canon of sacred Buddhist literature, this collection of some 550 anecdotes and fables depicts earlier incarnations — sometimes as an animal, sometimes as a human — of the being who would become Siddhartha Gautama, the future Buddha. Many of the tales are set in or near Benares, now called Varanasi, a city in north central India on the Ganges River. According to tradition, Buddha began his teaching at Sarnath a short distance from this city.

3. **Parables in Bible**: Parables make us think just as they did for those who heard it in the first century. We have to look at the image and see how that image works for us today. In the early church, Parables were interpreted as allegories. Parables were interpreted by way of searching the hidden meaning behind words. This is known as the "hardening theory" or the intention of the Bible to conceal the truth of God from non-believers. Thus, the Jerusalem is heaven in the Parable of Good Samaritan. Jericho is the world, robber is Satan, priest is religion, Levite is the church and Samaritan is Christ. Julicher was the first theologian to free parables from early allegorical interpretation. He argued for the scenery approach in interpreting parables. We should not read parables by the words and between the lines. Instead, we should see parable as a whole picture. In other words we should see a bird not the eyes, the wings and the feathers. It was A. T. Cadoux and later C.H. Dodd who laid down the principle that Parables are best interpreted in the setting of the life of Jesus Christ. This brings hermeneutic on the path to historical approach of the Parables.

4. **Aesop's Fables**: Aesop's Fables or the Aesopica are a collection of fables credited to Aesop, a slave and story-teller believed to have lived in ancient Greece between 620 and 560 BCE. A fable is a form of storytelling that usually features animals behaving like humans. The purpose of the fable is to teach a lesson about a

human weakness or folly. To reinforce this lesson, fables usually include a moral at the end of the tale. The true Fable, if it rise to its high requirements, ever aims at one great end and purpose representation of human motive, and the improvement of human conduct, and yet it so conceals its design under the disguise of fictitious characters, by clothing with speech the animals of the field, the birds of the air, the trees of the wood, or the beasts of the forest, that the reader shall receive advice without perceiving the presence of the adviser. Thus the superiority of the counsellor, which often renders counsel unpalatable, is kept out of view, and the lesson comes with the greater acceptance when the reader is led, unconsciously to himself, to have his sympathies enlisted in behalf of what is pure, honourable, and praiseworthy, and to have his indignation excited against what is low, ignoble, and unworthy. The true fabulist, therefore, discharges a most important function. He is neither a narrator, nor an allegorist. He is a great teacher, a corrector of morals, a censor of vice, and a commandeer of virtue. In this consists the superiority of the Fable over the Tale or the Parable. The fabulist is to create a laugh, but yet, under a merry guise, to convey instruction.

5. **Zen Stories**. Zen stories, or "koans".. are told with the express purpose of trying to get the listener to open their mind. Zen is a form of Buddhism that places emphasis on attaining awakening or the "path of enlightenment." It's used as a method of trying to discover the true meaning of life. Zen teaches its followers to strip away their "layers" - their expectations, opinions and even beliefs - so that they can see the truth of who they really are and what they really want in their lives. Zen encourages its practitioners to meditate to find their "Buddha-nature." It teaches that Buddha-nature is a natural state of wisdom and virtue that everyone has inside of them.

Reflections of an ELT Practitioner on Storytelling for Spiritual Education

Within the parameters of teachers' professional development, storytelling is seen as a way for teachers to inquire into their own knowledge and understanding of practice. Characterised as a narrative mode of intelligence (Bruner, 1986), storytelling is a way of thinking about experience that is situated in time and space and which values the individual's view of the world. Storytelling is linked to theoretical models of reflective learning (McDrury & Alterio, 2002) by enabling teachers to 'recapture their experience, think about it, mull it over and evaluate it' (Boud, Keogh, & Walker, 1985). More- over, several studies (Johnson & Golombek 2002; McDrury & Alterio, 2002; Ritchie & Wilson, 2000) demonstrate the capacity of storytelling to support reflective practice, identified as a professional attribute for teaching in Europe (Kelly et al., 2002; Training and Development Agency, 2007). Furthermore, storytelling is used as a way to empower teachers, giving them a voice to express emotion, create meaning and situate their teaching in a wider political context (Ritchie & Wilson, 2000).

In the context of *spiritual education* the role of the ELT teacher becomes a bit different. This was evidenced in this activity, when after the initial five stories many pre-service teachers felt *is it necessary to always state the moral of the story whenever we tell a story in class? Can't we allow our students to figure out what is the aim behind the story?* As Scott and Dinham (2008) have argued, "Teachers who are looking for ways to solve problems or make decisions in their classrooms are highly likely to prefer the example or advice of a colleague to the disembodied wisdom of a theory or set of empirical findings". This is one of the ways teachers engage with stories in the classroom. But, the essential aspect to remember, is that today, students in our classrooms are no longer interested in a *prescriptive* mode of discourse, instead, the discourse needs to gel the essence of the morality code without encroaching upon the degrees of freedom that the students in our class not only crave for but are constantly encouraged to exercise by the prevalent societal values. The role of the teacher becomes very challenging in this context: as teachers themselves have followed the *prescriptive regime of life* where they were *told* as to what is right and what is wrong when they were young adult yet now it is expected of them shed the prescriptive view and instead follow an approach that gives their students a sense of freedom to choose. But there is a flip side to this so *called approach to freedom.* For many students being prescriptive helps in formulating a value system for themselves as this in line with the traditions that are followed in majority of the Indian homes where the young adults are expected to follow certain traditions and practices. This prescriptive view is helpful, for this ultimately acts as the umbilical cord that joins that student with the family and in a way the entire society. The values and morals learnt within this view, act as anchors in the life that help the young adult not to commit follies rather be balanced towards their outlook in life.

If the aim of spiritual education is to allow the individual to realize nature of *self and* find ways to *nurture oneself,* the onus of the storyteller (in this case the ELT teacher) becomes very *spiritual* in itself. It becomes a *quest in itself,* where the teacher and the taught embark upon a journey that entails the discovery, rationalization, realisation and reflection at the level of the teacher and the taught, at the level of the storyteller and the story-listener.

Jon Meacham (2008) recently wrote "We are the sum of the stories we tell ourselves, and those stories are necessarily rooted in our experience, and by how we choose to interpret the experiences of others." Storytelling, the oldest of form of communication, provides us a means for reconstructing our experiences as well as constructing our inquiry into future professional practice. Thus, it would seem that this approach (storytelling) could serve as an improvement, or an effective supplement, to other techniques used by teachers in promoting value system and mechanisms to help the students to realize their own selves: which ultimately is what spiritual education is all about.

References

1. Boud, D., Keogh, R., & Walker, D. (1985). Reflection: Turning experience into learning. London: Kogan Page.
2. Bruner, J. (1987). Life as narrative. Social Research, 54, 13-32.
3. Dakhtin, M. (1981). Discourse in the novel. In M. Holquist (Ed.), The dialogic imagination: Four essays by M. M. Dakhtin. Austin, TX: University of Texas Press.
4. Dyson, A. H., & Genishi, C. (1994). The need for story: Cultural diversity in classroom and community. Urbana, IL: National Council of Teachers of English.
5. Flowers, B. S. (1988). Joseph Campbell: The power of myth with Bill Moyers. New York: Doubleday.
6. Johnson, K.E., & Golombek, P.R. (2002). Teachers' narrative inquiry as professional devel- opment. Cambridge: Cambridge University Press. Kelly, M., Grenfell, M., Gallagher-Brett, A., Jones, D., Richard, L., & Hilmarsson-Dunn, A. (2002). The training of teachers of a foreign language: Developments in Europe. A report to the European Commission Directorate General for Education and Culture. Retrieved from http://ec.europa.eu/education/languages/pdf/doc493 en.pdf
7. McDrury, J., & Alterio, M. (2002). Learning through storytelling in higher education: Using reflection and experience to improve learning. London: Kogan Page.
8. Meacham, J. (2008, July 7/July 14). The stories we tell ourselves. Newsweek, 27-28
9. Ritchie, J.S., & Wilson, D.E. (2000). Teacher narrative as critical inquiry. Rewriting the script. New York/London: Teachers College Press.
10. Scott, C., & Dinham, S. (2008). Born not made: The nativist myth and teachers' thinking. Teacher Development, 12(2), 115-124.
11. Shulman, L. (1987). Knowledge and teaching: Foundation of the new reform. Harvard Educational Review, 57(1), 1-22.
12. Stern, D. (1985). The interpersonal world of the infant: A view from psychoanalysis and developmental psychology. New York: Basic Books.
13. Training and Development Agency. (2007). Professional standards for teachers. Qualified teacher status. Retrieved from www.tda.gov.uk/ standards

14. Van Groenou, M. (1995, Summer). "Tell me a story": Using children's oral culture in a preschool setting. Montessori LIFE.
15. Zabel, M. K. (1991, Fall). Storytelling, myths, and folk tales: Strategies for multicultural inclusion. Preventing School Failure, 32.

CHAPTER–10

FOSTERING SPIRITUAL DEVELOPMENT THROUGH EDUCATION

Dr. Aradhana Mani,
Amity Institute of Education
Amity University, Noida, India

Spirituality is the "art and science of Divine remembrance." i.e., doing everything in the remembrance of God so that anything we do has a thought of divinity attached to it. This motivates us to keep the highest goals in all aspects of living and prevents us at all times from doing anything wrong. *Therefore it is necessary that our students are educated in spiritual values.*

Spiritual development is the development of a sense of identity, self-worth, personal insight, meaning and purpose. It is about the development of a pupil's 'spirit'. Some people may call it the development of a pupil's 'soul'; others as the development of 'personality' or 'character'. Human beings are endowed with spiritual capacities. Spiritual development is a difficult area to inspect. Effective provision for spiritual development depends on a curriculum and approaches to teaching which embody clear values and provide opportunities for pupils to gain understanding by developing a sense of curiosity through reflection on their own and other people's lives and beliefs, their environment and the human condition. It relies on teachers receiving and valuing pupils' ideas across the whole curriculum. Acts of worship play a particular part. To the extent that spiritual insights imply an awareness of how pupils relate to others, there is a strong link to both moral and social development.– *Handbook for the Inspection of Schools in Wales (OHMCI, Wales)*

A spiritual foundation, irrespective of a person's religion or value system, provides a deeper context to a child's activities, be it academic, physical, social, or professional. Such a focus helps children develop universal values and virtues such as trustworthiness, compassion, humility, courage, kindness, and patience in an effort to assist them to expand their ability to better perceive, participate, experience, empathize, and comprehend the world around them.

Spiritual development involves:

- the development of insights, principles, beliefs, attitudes and values which guide and motivate us. For many pupils, these have a significant religious basis
- a developing understanding of feelings and emotions which causes us to reflect and to learn
- for all pupils, a developing recognition that their insights, principles, beliefs, attitudes and values should influence, inspire or guide them in life.

Schools can encourage pupils' spiritual development by :

- giving pupils the opportunity to explore values and beliefs, including religious beliefs, and the way in which they affect peoples' lives
- supporting and developing the beliefs in ways which are personal and relevant to them

- encouraging pupils to reflect and learn from reflection
- giving pupils the opportunity to understand human feelings and emotions, the way they affect people and how an understanding of them can be helpful
- developing a climate or ethos within which all pupils can grow and flourish, respect others and be respected
- accommodating difference and respecting the integrity of individuals
- promoting teaching styles which value pupils' questions and give them space for their own thoughts, ideas and concerns
- enable pupils to make connections between aspects of their learning
- encourage pupils to relate their learning to a wider frame of reference – for example, asking 'why?', 'how?' and 'where?' as well as 'what?'"

What Influences the Religious and Spiritual Development of Students?

Culture

The mission and character of a school exerts significant influence on the spiritual journey of its students.

Curriculum

Academic programs also influence students' understanding of religion and the role of spirituality in providing a forum for self-discovery as well as academic development. Student enrollment in religion courses has helped students develop a more complex understanding of who they are and what they believe. But students do not always find sufficient support in their quest to find meaning and purpose in life in their academic pursuits.

Co-curriculum

Students who participate in religious activities are more apt to have stronger religious commitments than those who are not as involved. Similarly, students who are engaged in religious activities are also more apt to be engaged in other school activities. Their religious engagement is considered to be helpful in having a positive attitude towards their institution and developing themselves as whole persons, as well as being engaged in other activities.

Community

The relationships the students develop with others—fellow students, faculty and professionals in the campus play an important role in providing the often necessary social support for students throughout their school experience. The school administrators should encourage their faculty to assist students in developing their affective, spiritual, and religious dimensions as well as their cognitive and intellectual capacities.

How can classroom teaching bring about personal change in young people?

Schools must prepare students to accept their social responsibilities as members of a democratic society. Students must learn the knowledge and develop skills, values and attitudes which will enable them to contribute to society as active and informed and confident citizens.In addition to providing a basis for personal fulfilment and positive citizenship, the curriculum must aim to prepare students for a changing society. Generally, the aims for schools that go beyond the acquisition of knowledge and cognitive skills are expressed in terms of promoting the growth and development of the whole person- the idea of a holistic education.

Need of value based spiritual education

Parents, teachers, family, school, environment, friends, society, religion - all these wield a great influence on the child.Physical deviations – games, yoga, dance, gymnastics etc. All these help to teach them the values for life. Academics and Co-curricular activities both help in teaching values. Meditation, Value Based Education, Music, Self analysis, Positive affirmations and Resolutions help in improving our character. The suggestions and words spoken by the parents and others affect the character and good conduct of a child. The "learned teachers" are like sign posts by the road, to tell you where the road leads to.

Approaches to Value Based Spiritual Education

Independent approach inculcates values in a deliberate manner more effectively through specific, special time slots allotted in the time table .It includes-

- Teacher directed activities
- Individual activities by students
- Group activities like games, exhibitions, discussions, role-play, debates, dramatization, making collages etc.

Integrated Approach is a recent development, where the common spiritual and behavioural values are taught, while a course is being taught. This means that each and every teacher who teaches a course must incorporate values in each of the topic

Integration is possible in both curricular and co-curricular courses.

In this integrated approach, the student will neither forget the course nor the value. For example, while teaching about pendulum and motion, it can be correlated to mind, desires and contentment.

Teaching of science should get humanized, e.g.; In the lessons of human physiology/biology, heart and brain should be studied not simply as pumping stations and memory control towers but as seats of love, feelings, emotions, conscience – the qualities that mankind is characterised by.

Subtle Approach

The most effective, though difficult to comprehend or integrate. It is based on the fact that "Values are caught and not taught". Parents, teachers, peers, family and society influence the student and his behaviour. Parents and teachers must regulate their minds. Parents have to be wise enough to know that "My child is mine; nevertheless it has its own existence. It has a tendency of growth and let me allow it grow".

Actions speak louder than words. Students learn values from **What we are** than from **What we say**. They also pick up hidden and unintended values from *what is **said** and **not said**. what is **done** and **not done!***

A teacher who approaches any subject with love, wins over the hearts of his/her wards. Love is the catalyst which grooms the pupils into complete human beings.

Conclusion

Education today should cater to an individual's intellectual, physical, emotional, social and spiritual development. Education should help him/her evolve into a person with holistic vision and growth, culminating in preparing a happy future for an integrated mankind. The need of the hour is to educate the student community on the need for spirituality in their life and for that; the educators themselves must be role models. It is earnestly hoped that academic institutions interested in imparting value based spiritual education work in collaboration with a non-profit, purely spiritual organisation for training their teachers who in turn will train their students.

References

Agneta, U.(2005). Different Strategies Concerning Multiculturality

Retrieved from: http://www.ethicseducationforchildren.org/news/en_US/2005/12/13/01/different-strategies-concerning-multiculturality

Braskamp, L. A. (2007). Fostering Religious and Spiritual Development of Students during College

Retrieved from: http://religion.ssrc.org/reforum/Braskamp.pdf

Crawford,M. & Rossiter, G. (1992). Teaching Wisdom: Religious Education and the Moral and Spiritual Development of Young People. Retrieved from: *http://203.10.46.30/ren2/gr17.html*

Handbook for the Inspection of Schools in Wales. (1999). British Humanist Association, London.

Ingersoll, R.E& Bauer,A.L. (2004). An integral approach to spiritual wellness in school counseling settings.Retrieved from: http://findarticles.com/p/articles/mi_m0KOC/is_5_7/ai_n6121235/

Krishna, P. (2008).Education in Values- Strategies and Challenges for Value Education

Retrieved from: http://cce.iisc.ernet.in/nsee/Presentation/7

CHAPTER–11

Spiritual Development: Need of the Hour

Dr. Manisha Minocha,
Principal,
KIRAS, New Delhi

Dr. Monica Auplish,
Assistant Professor,
KIRAS, New Delhi

Today, all of us experience feelings of loneliness, depression, helplessness and hopelessness from time to time; Children today have to face a variety of situations in their daily lives: situations that cause stress and anxiety. The most common sources of day to day stress these days are:-

1) Problems with peers
2) Family issues
3) School related problems
4) Pressures from one's own thoughts, feelings or behavior

These types of problems lower one's self esteem self confidence and sense of worth. All of us have to face some or the other type of crisis. As all of us are unique therefore, the way of responding to the crisis is different. In considering whether a person may be suicidal, it is imperative that the crisis should be evaluated from each person's perspective. What may seem of minor importance to one may be insignificant or may be distressful to another.

There is empirical evidence that "youth and the middle aged between 30 and 44 years are the prime groups taking recourse of path of suicide. Of the total suicide victims, around 37.6 per cent are youth in the age group of 14 to 30 years".

In this modern age, children are not brought up in a peaceful atmosphere. There is a lot of pressure from school, society, peer group, parents and teachers. The truth is the education system has not served its purpose. Being unable to express emotions, putting on a facade of sociability and living a life that is more pretension than reality, has alienated us from the world and made us a prisoner of our own dreams. In the last few years youngsters especially in urban areas have been facing the problem of stress and competition. The reasons range between

i) Aspirations of parents that are unrealistic

ii) Failure or stress of relationships

iii) A competitive society

iv) Mismatch between cultural values and

v) Socio economic aspirations.

Children need to be prepared to handle the pressures. We are in a transitory phase and children have to discover themselves before stepping into the competitive world. We are moving from a traditional society to one that is westernized. Values are changing from the spiritual to the materialistic. The urban life style is leading to crimes. Relationships are breaking down due to intense rivalries, frustration and anger. Indiscipline is growing in the schools and is becoming a leading cause of concern for teachers. There is a growing feeling of alienation and loneliness. It is not sufficient for parents, teachers and other adults to understand the problem of knowledge regarding the ways, means and devices of controlling and managing their emotions and feelings.

Spiritual Development

Spiritual development according to Thompson and Randall (1999)

"Concerns the broad search for transcendental meaning that may be as simple as a young child's inquiries into how the world came into being or as complex as a theologian's metaphysical analysis"

The main concerns of spiritual development are

(a) The metaphysical

(b) Values

(c) Religious practices and symbols

There is a reflection aspect of spiritual development that is concerned with a vision of the purpose of existence and ultimate reasons for living a moral life. It is concerned with -

Who am I?
Why am I in this world? What is my future?
What is right and what is wrong?
Why is there wrong in this world?
Why should I act rightly?
Why is there suffering in the world?
Why is forgiveness important?
Why should I have love and compassion for others?

The meaning of spirituality differs for different individuals, but for all people it implies formation of a connection with something that is greater than oneself. The spiritual development of a child is often equated with some level of social development or psychological development.

Besides solving the problem of stress and providing a meaning and direction of life for people spiritual development is needed in the

21st century for many other reasons. Spiritual development contributes towards the development of certain qualities which will make the world a place of peaceful co-existence. These qualities are:

1) Forgiveness
2) Compassion and kindness towards all fellow beings
3) Patience
4) Understanding, knowledge and wisdom
5) Self awareness and self acceptance
6) Fearlessness towards life and death
7) Truthfulness

Forgiveness is a form of spiritual development of a person. Spiritual behavior involves letting go of hurt, ill will towards another person or persons, which is a form of attachment to worldly feelings. It would be a large step towards world

peace and happiness if we accept the sincerity of regret expressed by a person. Even if the other person does not express regret or ask for forgiveness it is required for one's own peace of mind. Lack of forgiveness harms a person in many ways. Harboring a grudge makes a person unhappy and he may chronically be seeking revenge and trying to payback the other person. The person becomes stressed and may harm himself, which is again an undesirable development. Developing a personal spirituality means one always trusts in goodness of others and believes in one's own good deeds. Forgiveness is beneficial for a person's individual happiness as well as for the well being of humanity as a whole, and the best way to develop the capacity and strength required to forgive others is through spiritual development.

Fostering spiritual growth in children

We should remain close to reality while taking the child towards spirituality. The child should be allowed to seek the truth rather than only listening to myths and legends. The child needs to understand

'Why' and not just believe for the sake of believing. They need to know the reasons for being truthful or loving towards others.

The child should be given opportunities to participate in religious ceremonies and discourses. These religious activities should be sometimes intergenerational and occasionally cater to the needs of children alone.

The child needs to be made to practice relationships which involve trust and empathic understanding towards others. He should be given support during periods of difficulty, crises or personal despair which will teach him to support others during such times.

The child should be assisted in his personal search for his identity and for understanding the world by engaging constructively with him in questioning and exploring more deeply the beliefs and culture taught to him by parents and teachers, in the process of socialization.

References

F.K. Oser & W.G.Scarlet (Eds.), Religious Development in Childhood and Adolescence

Harper Collins, J.W.Fowler (1991), Stages in Faith Consciousness, New York

J.W.Fowler (1981), Stages of faith, New York

Minocha, Manisha, Educational and Vocational Guidance, Arya Book Depot, 2008

Thompson, R.A. & Randall, B (1999), A Standard of Living Adequate for Children's Spiritual Development

Section-C

VALUE, EDUCATION AND SPIRITUALITY

CHAPTER–12

VALUE OF EDUCATION VIS-À-VIS VALUE EDUCATION: Swami Vivekananda's Fundamental Thoughts on Education and their Practical Application in the Present-day Context

Swami Atmapriyananda,
Vice Chancellor,
Ramakrishna Mission Vivekananda University
PO Belur Math, Dist Howrah, West Bengal

1. Value of Education vs. Value Education

Let us begin with three beautiful stories. One is from Sri Ramakrishna's *Gospel*, the second from *Chhandogya Upanishad* and the third from Roger Penrose's *Emperor's New Mind.*

1.1. P*arable in Sri Ramakrishna's Gospel*

A highly educated pundit was travelling in a boat. He was parading his knowledge before the fellow travellers, who were looking on with wonder. The 'uneducated' helmsman was one of the admirers. The pundit would question him now and then: 'Hey, have you studied the philosophy of the *sankhya*?' The helmsman would say in dismay:

'No, Sir, I know nothing of philosophy.' 'Ah', the pundit would say, 'you have wasted a quarter of your life, poor fellow.' Again he would ask: 'Do you know anything about yoga?' 'O no, Sir' would be the reply, to which the pundit would say with a chuckle: 'Half of your life is gone—useless and without value'. 'What about some Vedanta, man?' would be the next question. And the gentle boatman would say: 'I have no idea at all, Sir'. 'Well, three-fourths of your life has already gone a waste. What value does life have without the knowledge of Vedanta, eh?' Just at that time there was a storm. The gale wind began to rock the boat violently. Everybody including the pundit began to panic. The helmsman asked the pundit anxiously: 'Sir, can you swim?' 'No' replied the scholar. The ignoramus of a helmsman quipped gently: 'Sir, now that the boat is about to capsize, your *whole* life is gone! I may not know *sankhya, yoga or Vedanta*, but I know how to swim!'

The message coming from this simple story is powerfully telling: what is the value of our knowledge, our education, our scholarship, if it cannot help us swim across the current of life, to face and conquer the gales and storms that should inevitably come to everyone in the course of life? Shankara's famous hymn, with the burden: *tatah kim, tatah him, tatah him, tatah him* (meaning 'what of that, what avails it, so what, what thence') comes to mind in this context. What is the value of all our 'boast of heraldry and pomp of power', our knowledge and education, if they fail us when we need them most—in the hours of crises? We pride ourselves as being highly 'educated', but drown helplessly, 'unwept, unhonoured and unsung' in the currents and crosscurrents, in the whirlpools and eddies of life. What is the value of that education that cannot provide us with the strength to encounter and withstand a thunderstorm in the course of our life?

1.2. *Narada-Sanatkumara dialogue in the Chhandogya Upanishad*

Narada, the highly educated scholar, goes to Sanatkumara, illumined sage, to unburden the agony of his soul. (Refer *Chhandogya Upanishad,*

Chapter VII, Section 1). Narada is restless, he does not have peace of mind, and he feels unfulfilled and lost. He approaches Sanatkumara and humbly requests to be taught. Sanatkumara replies: 'First tell me in detail all that you have studied so far. I would then be able to teach you further.' Narada then gives a huge list of things he has already mastered. He then adds in humble desperation: 'Sir, with all this knowledge that I have acquired, I feel I have merely become learned in plenty of *words and formulae*; I have not known the Self, the Atman, that is the Source of all knowledge. I have heard from men of wisdom like you that he who realizes the Self overcomes sorrow. I am deeply afflicted with sorrow. Venerable Sir, kindly be gracious enough to help me cross over to the other shore of the ocean of misery.' The compassionate guru, Sanatkumara, then utters a powerful one-liner: 'Whatever you have studied is only a *name*'. One is reminded of Sri Ramakrishna's telling example: the almanac predicts that there shall be so much rainfall. But then squeeze the book and you will not get a single drop!

This Upanishadic story once again emphasizes the same truth—of what value is our education if it cannot take us beyond sorrow, beyond the anguish and the ennui of the soul eating into our very vitals? Herein lies the urgency of that education, of that knowledge, that would help us discover the real value of all that we study and perceive.

1.3. *Roger Penrose's Prologue in his book Emperor's New Mind*

The greatest super computer in the world is being inaugurated—a machine that could handle several billion calculations in a microsecond. Pose any problem, and it would not even be a split of a nanosecond before the answer is flashed on the screen. Among the audience are scientists, mathematicians, engineers, bureaucrats, political heavyweights and of course, the inventor of this super-intelligence. The President of the country is getting ready to inaugurate. The inaugural ceremony consists in asking the first question of this super machine and the prerogative should naturally go to the honourable members of the audience. "Who will put the first question?" the inaugurator quips. All the wise men of science and engineering among the audience look at one another in dismay. Who would be so foolish as to expose one's ignorance before this mighty giant, this near-omniscience never before known to humankind? The silence was broken by a shrieking voice of a little boy. "May I put the first question, sir?" asked the boy. "O come on" said the inaugurator, hardly hiding his smile at the innocence of this foolish little boy. The boy smartly asked: "What does it feel to be a computer?" The super computer began to respond. Its lights—red, yellow and orange—began to blink and wink. Seconds passed, minutes passed and it was more than an hour. The computer went on and on and on with its elaborate calculations and finally the answer flashed on the screen: "I don't know". The entire audience burst into laughter, giggling and chuckling at the plight of this super-intelligence unable to answer a simple question.

Penrose was arguing against the blind ally of algorithmic thinking by the human brain. He was building up a case against the so-called artificial intelligence (AI) and against the so-called strong AI protoganists. The man-vs-machine conflict as exemplified the Kasparov-vs-Deep Blue fight for superiority is a wonderful modern re-enactment of the Puranic *Bhasmasura* story—one who endows the *asura* with superior power is himself threatened to be destroyed at the hands of this power! Human civilization is desperately struggling to create super machines at whose hands it threatens to get vanquished and ultimately annihilated.

2. Character—the Sum and Substance of Value Education

We celebrated the golden jubilee of our independence some years ago. But whether we have been able to free ourselves from the psychology of dependence is as many years is a question, whose answer, alas, is no. 'What is lacking? O what is lacking?' is one question that is a subject of perennial discussion everywhere, and by everybody—from the Parliament to the market-place, by the country's top leaders down to the man in the street. We seem to be advancing in all spheres. Then why are we in this appalling state of affairs? What is lacking in us? The answer is quite simple: 'character'.

Character appears a rather simplistic virtue. Of course, it is really a very simple virtue. Indeed, all great truths are simple because simplicity is the hallmark of greatness. But then, simplicity seems to be the most difficult thing to acquire, much less to practise. It appears simple because it is not so much acquired as it is *discovered* in the core of one's being. It is our very essence, as fundamental to us as our very existence. There are two simple characteristics of a person who is endowed with impeccable character. Both of them owe their origin to Sri Ramakrishna's sayings:

1) "Keep your speech and mind in unison" (in Bengali he would say, "*man much ek karo*"). This is in fact an echo of the Vedic mantra: *vang me mani pratisthita; mano me vachi pratishthitam*).
2) "Do not allow perjury in the sacred shrine of your heart" (in original Bengali: "*bhaver ghare churi karo na*").

These two together would mean: (1) Speak what you deeply think and feel to be true; and do what you actually speak. (2) Allow no deception in your thought, word and action. In modern language, be absolutely **transparent**. The illustration of *sphatika*, the beautiful, transparent substance, is well known in our scriptures to describe the mind of a person who has been established in this virtue.

Character building is the aim and end of all education, according to Swami Vivekananda. His educational vision needs to be re-emphasized and re-focussed, if our present-day educational system is to survive the shock of collapse into mediocrity. Swami Vivekananda's fundamental thoughts on education, with hints on their practice and application are given below. These form the core of the philosophy of Ramakrishna Mission's educational institutions, which have been created to experiment with and actualize Vivekananda's thoughts.

3. Swami Vivekananda's Fundamental Thoughts on Education including their Practice and Application:

(The words under quotation marks are Swami Vivekananda's original words, while the rest is a paraphrase of his ideas).

1) Education is not mere accumulation of information. "We must have life-building, man-making, character-making assimilation of ideas. If you have assimilated five ideas and made them your life and character, you have more education than any man who has got by heart a whole library."
2) 'Education is the manifestation of the perfection already in man." It is the manifestation of the potential perfection, the infinite possibilities of the human soul, for which the teacher and the environment act merely as catalysts. "Vedanta says that within man is all knowledge and it requires only an awakening, and that much is the work of a teacher. You cannot teach a child any more than you can grow a plant."
3) "Mere book learning won't do. We want that education by which character is formed, strength of mind is increased, the intellect is expanded, and by which one can stand on one's own feet."
4) "The training by which the current and expression of will are brought under control and become fruitful is called education."
5) "We have but one method of acquiring knowledge, and that method is what is called concentration. There is no limit to the power of the human mind. The more concentrated it is, the more power is brought to bear on one point; that is the secret. This, the power of concentration, is the only key to the treasure house of knowledge. To me the very essence of education is the concentration of mind, not the collecting of facts."
6) "Along with the development of concentration we must develop the power of detachment. We must learn not only to attach the

mind to one thing exclusively, but also to detach it at a moment's notice and place it upon something else. This the systematic development of the mind."

7) Students should be taught the glorious spiritual and cultural heritage of our country. "We must have a hold on the spiritual and secular education of the nation. We must have the whole education of our country, spiritual and secular, in our hands, and it must be on national lines, through national methods, as far as practical."

8) The personal life of the teacher is one of the most powerful influences on the student. "One should live from his very boyhood with one whose character is like a blazing fire, and should have before him a living example of the highest teaching. In our country, the imparting of knowledge has always been through men of renunciation. The charge of imparting knowledge should again fall upon the shoulders of *tyagis*."

9) Indian spiritual idealism must be combined with Western science and technology to tackle comprehensively the problems of life. "What we need is to study, independent of foreign control, different branches of knowledge that are our own, and with it the English language and Western science; we need technical education and all else which may develop industries, so that men, instead of seeking for service, may earn enough to provide for themselves."

10) Education should be productive of human good. Every educated man and woman should strive for the uplift of the masses. "The greatest national sin is the neglect of the masses. ... They pay for our education; we must work for them." "So long as the millions live in hunger and ignorance, I hold every man a traitor, who, having been educated at their expense, pays not the least heed to them."

11) True religion or spirituality should be the prime motive force in the process of education. "I look upon religion as the innermost core of education." "We are the children of the Almighty, we are sparks of the infinite, divine Fire. ... teach this

life-saving, great, ennobling, grand doctrine to your children, even from their very birth."

12) "True education is gained by constant living in communion with Nature."

13) "The true teacher is he who can immediately come down to the level of the student, and transfer his soul to the student's soul and see through his eyes and understand through his mind. Such a teacher can really teach and none else. The conditions necessary for the taught are purity, a real thirst for knowledge, and perseverance. Purity in thought, speech and act is absolutely necessary."

Some of the practices successfully adopted in Ramakrishna Mission's educational institutions to actualize the above educational thoughts of Swami Vivekananda are briefly mentioned below *seriatim*:

1) That the aim of education is not mere book learning or accumulation of vast amounts of information is impressed upon the students from the very start of the courses. They are shown the ills of having cartloads of information without seriously assimilating any of them through such simple methods as framing questions that need penetrative thinking rather than mere cramming of information. They are taught the lives of great men and women with outstanding character energy, those who reshaped the history and destiny of humankind, although not 'educated' in the sense of passing examinations or securing degrees. The idea that passion for knowledge, undivided focus on an idea and assimilation of the ideas being taught are the prerequisites of education, is being inculcated in the students through the lives of great scientists and men of letters like Srinivasa Ramanujan, Marie Curie, Rabindranath Tagore etc. Eminent persons in various fields of science, arts and social sciences interact periodically with the students to inspire them with the educational ideals.

2) By teaching them the Vedantic doctrine of the infinite power and glory residing in the Self, the Atman, which is the innermost core of one's being, the students are taught self-esteem, self-

reverence and self-confidence. Independent thinking, rather than overmuch dependence on outside resources, is encouraged. Free discussions, debates and expression of views through various fora bring out the inner potentiality of the student. An atmosphere of freedom together with strict discipline is sought to be maintained.

3) Expansion of intellect and increase of mental strength come through a wide range of interactions and through wide reading about various peoples, their cultures and civilizations. Practical fieldwork and falling back upon one's own inner resources in trying situations are the means for developing a strong mind and a powerful will. The students are always taught to think positive, elevating thoughts and not be carried away by all the negative projections especially by the media.

4) To help the students to bring under control the current and expression of their will, small practices like fasting on fixed days, denying simple necessities which they are used to, keeping night vigil on some special occasions in order to overcome sleep etc are taught. Vow of silence (*mouna-vrata*) for some fixed period is also a great help in the exercise of speech control. The secret is to make them get a taste of self-conquest and self-mastery.

5) Teaching the students some practices in order to help them develop concentration through (i) observance of strict *brahmacharya* while one is a student (*antevasin*) (ii) keen observation of one's own mental gyrations and extrovert tendencies with a view to calming the mental waves (iii) constant *vichara* (discrimination) about their inner thinking and outer activities. To test out their level of concentration in practical life, some simple exercises may be given, like quoting from memory certain elevating passages after reading them only a few times, quick responses to questions on topics that they might have studied only a few times before. Further, telling them some inspiring anecdotes from the lives of great men, not only from the spiritual field (like Swami Vivekananda and Shankaracharya's phenomenal memory—they were called *srutidharas*), but also from the so-called secular field like Napolean etc. is a great help.

6) To develop detachment, encourage the students to give up certain common things which they are used to. Ask them to restrain for some fixed period from communicating, either verbally or in writing, with people dear to them. Encourage them to give away some of their possessions that they hold very dear, like a pen, a shirt, books etc.

7) The glory and power of our hoary spiritual heritage should be taught to the students through regular classes, dramas, film/video shows, exhibitions etc. They should be encouraged to commit to memory some of the immortal verses from the Gita, the Upanishads, Mahabharata, the teachings of great saints etc. A sense of pride in our rich heritage and ancient wisdom should be inculcated in the students by showing them how these principles and truths are in perfect accord with modern science and by exposing them to the statements of scientists like Eddington, Einstein etc. Besides, they should also be encouraged to study books showing the parallels between Vedanta and modern science.

8) Unless the teachers show a sense of dedication, self-sacrifice, deep love for their pupils, lack of greed etc, mere talk will never influence the students. A suitable congenial atmosphere should be created and proper teachers should be recruited for this to be possible. If at least some of the teachers are men of blazing character, they would help to mould the lives of students in a big way.

9) Swami Vivekananda wrote to one of his disciples: "Can you become an Occidental of occidentals in your spirit of equality, freedom, working energy, and at the same time a Hindu to the very backbone in religious culture and instincts? This is to be done and we will do it." By this Swamiji meant that we should combine the best elements of the Occident and the Orient, West and the East, Western scientific temper and Eastern inward contemplation. Then alone could we make men of all-round character, calm, contemplative, *sattvik* in their outlook, pious, noble, forbearing and peaceful, and at the same time, persevering, tenacious in approach, bold, daring, aggressively good (in

contrast to being passively good), efficient, hard-working, intensely practical and endowed with scientific, rational outlook. Our students should be trained in such a manner that they would delve deep into their inner consciousness at the time of prayer and meditation, and work like lions with girded loins in the field of action. They should be made to be proficient in both English and Sanskrit. Such a proficiency would open the doors of both the modern and ancient worlds, making for a wonderful combination. At the same time, they should have technical skill and proficiency.

10) To make the students feel for their unfortunate and underprivileged brethren, they should be made to work in the slum areas, in villages, mixing freely with the rural people, with the uneducated men and women there, and try to help them in all possible ways. Regular free coaching classes of slum children etc could be easily arranged.

11) Unfortunately, in this land of religion and spirituality, the words 'religion' and 'God' are becoming taboos. If the Vedantic religion and philosophy could be revived and taught in modern language, this taboo could be easily removed. For, Vedanta teaches the two important doctrines of (i) divinity of all beings—the same Infinite Self or Atman resides in everyone, and (ii) oneness of existence (or solidarity of the universe). Vedantic religion, therefore, is free from all dogma, creed, narrow bigotry and any specific religious doctrine. It is scientific, rational, and elevating, for it tells everyone, from the lowest worm to the highest angel that he is a Divine Being, though encased in a limited body and a conditioned mind. This brings hope and develops a positive outlook in the life of a student. Swami Vivekananda believed and taught that Vedanta would be the future religion of thinking, rational humanity. The more these broad, life-giving principles of Vedanta are taught to students, the more would they become strong, positive, elevated in thinking and powerful in their inner convictions.

12) Our present system of education has taken the students and teachers far away from Nature. Study of Nature, what to speak

of communion, has become a rarity. The result is there for all to see. There is an alarming lack of Nature-awareness. Environmentalists all the world over are deeply concerned about this trend and are trying to reverse it by developing environmental awareness. The simplest way of doing this is to go back to our ancient method of encouraging the students to 'commune' with Nature, observe, watch, appreciate and get absorbed in the beauty of flowers and plants, animals and insects, rivers and ponds, stars and planets, the sun and the moon. A sense of wonder, a feeling of awe at the majesty and beauty of Nature, a profound emotion of gratitude for all the rich wealth of resources that Nature is giving us unasked and in boundless abandon—these higher sentiments are among the greatest assets of an educated person.

13) The pre-requisites and the qualifications necessary for both the teacher and the taught have been beautifully spelt out in our ancient scriptures and re-emphasized in modern times by prophets and saints like Sri Ramakrishna and Swami Vivekananda. An awareness of these will engender in both the teacher and the student a genuine striving to acquire and achieve these qualities and endow them with mutual respect. Just as the disciple should have *shraddha* in the guru, the guru too should have *shraddha* and love for the disciple. Such an atmosphere of mutual *shraddha*, love and respect would be the most harmonious for the cultivation of knowledge and wisdom. Only then the Vedic prayer: *tejasvinavadhitamastu, ma vidvishavahai,* (may our learning be illuminative and powerful; may there be no disharmony between us) would become meaningful.

Om Shantih, Shantih, Shantih. (Om Peace, peace, peace.)

CHAPTER–13

Towards a New era of Value Creation by Dr Diasaku Ikeda, President Soka Gakkai International

Dr. Sadhana Srivastava,
New Greenfield School, New Delhi

Introduction

We are living in an era marked by an absence of values, in which no measure of worth than the monetary is recognized. We need to develop the awareness that the standard of values that judges human worth solely on the basis of economic capacity represent the effective absence of values.

Human Security

The impact of current economic crisis on the more vulnerable members of society has been particularly severe .There are growing concern that new humanitarian crises may arise in different part of the world unless targeted assistance addressing the needs of these populations is provided. Three concrete areas where measures should be taken concern employment, children, and the empowerment of women.

In all these efforts, the key is the power of dialog and engagement to awaken that which is best in each individual. Just as there is no easy path to learning, there is no easy path to the realization of good. We must root ourselves firmly in reality ,deliberately taking on difficult challenges, ceaselessly training and forging ourselves in the "smelting furnace" of spiritual struggle and earnest engagement with others.

There is always a way, a path to the peak of even the most towering and forbidding mountain. What is more strongly required of us is the imagination that can appreciate the present crises as an opportunity to fundamentally transform the direction of history.

This must be a key function of religion to help people replant their feet firmly in the here and now, enabling an out-of-control civilization to realize its needed course correction. The here and now is the foundation and pivot of all aspects of human activities If we loose sight of this and base ourselves in a virtual world we end up the slaves of the very technologies that we ourselves created.

Towards a New era of value Creation by Dr Diasaku Ikeda, President Soka Gakkai International

As American president Obama himself noted in his noble Pease Prize acceptance speech:

"The non-violence practiced by men like Gandhi and King may not have been practical or possible in all circumstances, but the love that they preached –their fundamental faith in human progress- that must always be the North Star that guides us on our journey."

Indeed as Gandhi noted"Good teavels at a snail's pace" it is therefore vital to maintain an approach that is both flexible and persistent.

The greatest driving force for development of modern civilization has been science and technology.Yoshiharu Izumi is a scientist who has been exploring the relationship between religion, Buddhism in particular and science. He writes"Humanity has sought a stable and secure way of life, with religion serving as steering wheel and breaks to guide and counterbalance the accelerator of desire that stokes an engine of intellect".

Language and Values of Good

The essential characteristics of humanity that is virtue, nobility, honor, honesty, generosity has become almost impossible. We need to revive the human spirit and reawaken ordinary citizen, exhorting people to choose the good that is fruit of self mastery and resist the destructive pitfalls of evil.

We need to make an attempt to realize a fundamental transformation in human priorities based on the idea that a change in the destiny of a single individual can change the destiny of all humankind. When science and technology are divorced from the question of value, they are subject to no real control and potentially pose a deadly peril to human society .If this tendency is left unchecked, the consequences for humanity could be truly dire.

It is an unchanging conviction that source of energy to create value and open the door to new era is to be formed in religion. There is a need for the kind of religion that is compatible with and embraces the insights of science but can serve to guide and restrain those technologies that if misused, have a potential to wreak devastation on human kind.

If we can look beyond the diverse directions of daily life we will discover an innate capacity to appreciate genuine reality, to hear the heart beat of that which is truly worth living for.

Focus on the Here and Now

I was struck by the following words from an interview with a Japanese literary critic Shozo Kajima :"Only the here and now is the true reality …We only need to be passionate about here and now. If a person has aged in their feelings, they are old whatever their physical age. "Regarding the tendency of modern civilization to seek abundance and happiness outside ourselves. Kajima urges us to "awaken to the richness of the unrealized capacities we already possess within".

The phrase "here and now" is reminiscent to the proverb "Dig beneath your feet, there you will find a spring," and also an statement by Einstein: "my eternity is now I have only one interest: to fulfill my purpose here where I am.

This shares a deep commonality with the worldview of Buddhism. Core concepts of Mahamaya Buddhism _the simultaneity of cause and effect, the correspondence of the infinite past and later day of the law, instantaneous enlightment means attaining Buddhahood in one's present form.

The present may seem to be nothing more than an instant in the flow from the past toward the future. But in this present instant is a genuine reality that comprises the infinite past and the limitless future. That reality is the font of life's deepest and most essential strength. and it is this strength that while being constrained by the past, brings fort new hope for the future.

In this sense, now is the starting point of everything. The here and now is the foundation and pivot, the alpha and omega, of all aspects of human activity. If we loss sight of this and base ourselves in a virtual world, we end up the slaves of the very technologies which we ourselves created, oscillating uncontrollably between euphoric economic bubbles and despairing panics. Reality will be eroded and consumed by its virtual counterpart. A key function of religion to help people replant their feet firmly in the here and now, enabling an out -of –control civilization to realize its needed course correction.

In the Buddhist tradition, the path of the bodhisattva is a way of life dedicated to social engagement. It is rooted in sense of oneness with the cosmos, while at the same time being committed to courageous action and the project of "living well" from now into the future.

Einstein, in calling for a cosmic religious feeling, manifested a universal conscience and character as he dedicated himself for activated for peace. In like manner, the pioneer who stands along struggling to transfer history is focused on the present moment, vitally engaged with creation of value in the moment. Such person is propelled by the irresistible impulses of conscience and, from within the rich spectrum of spatial-temporal possibilities comprised in the present moment, carefully and courageously selects and generates the language and values of good.

Just as there is no easy path to learning, there no easy path to realization of good. We have no choice but to root ourselves firmly in reality, deliberately taking of difficult challenges, ceaselessly training and forging ourselves in the smelting furnace of the soul. This is the correct path to attainment of good.

As Marcel noted, there is always a tension between "the individuality of the circumstances and the universality of the law." He considered this tension " the crux, the spring" of value. In the teachings of Buddhism we find the words, the shallow is easy to embrace, but the profound is difficult. To discard the shallow and seek the profound is the way to courage." .This phrase shines as an enduring guide for life.

To pass through this tension ,this smelting furnace ,without error requires the willingness to seek the depths, to strengthen and brace oneself, day by day, month after month. Here we find the tautness of heart that enables us to turn away from the natural human tendency to seek the easy way out,and instead,day by day,to pursue the ideal ,training and evaluating oneself.

Ultimately all things are impermanent; reality is an endless succession of transformations. There is an expression to the effect that if you have not seen someone for three days, await your next encounter with a sense of anticipation. In other words, a person who is growing and developing will show some sign of change in the course of just three days. Those who possess the spirit to seek out the depths will not overlook these changes, but will respond to them with acuity, never ceasing the advance toword value creation.

Such words as hope ,courage, effort friendship and kindness naturally describe the qualities required to those who seek to break through present difficulties toward a better future. So process of contemplation, self-questioning and soul-searching to ensure that one's decisions are an expression of an inner stirring and motivation of he conscience.

When people of faith succumb to the impulse to blindly rely on and give all responsibility to forces outside ourselves, religion indeed becomes a kind of opium. In such a state ,it cannot support people in the pursuit of a way of life-described in Buddhism as the bodhisattva way-as proactive, self-reliant agents of change, transforming the era.

The choices and decisions of people who aspire to the good will demonstrate immense variety depending on their here and now. But it is the spirit seeking the depths and striving to strengthen itself that enables us to carry out our determination, neither avoiding nor escaping those circumstances.

It is imperative that we always resist the temptation to abandon dialog and adopt violence in its place. We must remain committed to the process of philosophical hesitation, enduring tension and the smelting furnace of ceaseless spiritual struggle ;for this is the one place where our humanity can be truly forged.

The existence of others is the inescapable premise for a genuinely humane way of life. The process of patiently, persistently training and strengthening ourselves demands that we confront and engage in dialogue with others. Our willingness and capacity to coexist peacefully with those who are different from us that which divides barbarity and civilization.

Contributive Way of Life

We must remember that there is always a way, a path to the peak of even the most towering and forbidding mountain. Even when a sheer rock face looms before us ,we should refuse to be disheartened, but instead continue the patient search for a way forward. In this sense, what is most strongly required of us is imagination that can appreciate the present crisis as an opportunity to fundamentally transform the direction of history. By mustering the force of inner will and determination we can convert challenges into the fuel for positive change.

When the Soka Gakkai was founded in 1930,Japan and world were shuddering under the impact of the financial panic of the previous year. People were afflicted by a deepening sense of dread and unease. Writing at that time the founder of the organization,Tsunesaburo Makiguchi(1871-1944),called a contributive way of life.He rejected a passive, dependent way of life in which one is swayed by and at the mercy of one,s surroundings and conditions of the times. He likewise rejected a way of life in which we are capable of looking out for our own needs but remain indifferent to the sufferings of others.

He urges, instead a contributive way of life as described by Buddhist maxim that when we light a lantern for others, our own way forward is lit. The source of illumination needed to dispel the chaos and dark-ness of the age to be found in actions that bring fourth our own inner light through committed action on behalf of others.

The second president of the Soka Gakkai, Josai Toda(1900-58),as heir to Makiguchi's spirit, declared :"I wish to see the word 'misery' no longer used to describe the world, any country, any individual." He put his conviction into practice through his efforts dedicated to peace and people's happiness and to the construction of popular solidarity rooted in a philosophy of respect for the sanctity of life and the dignity of the human person.

Surveying the challenges that confront contemporary global society, I am convinced that nothing is more crucial that an essential reorientation of our way of life based on commitment to the welfare of all of humankind and the entire planet, such as Makiguchi and Toda called for. Rather than stand to one side and ponder how the future might develop, we must focus on what each of us can do at this critical moment,the role each of us can choose to play in changing the direction of history. We must strive to make a proactive contributive way of life the prevailing spirit of the new era.

Reference

Ikeda, Daisaku, Towards A New Era of Value Creation, 2010 Peace Proposal, SGI, 15-3 Samoncho, Shinjuku-ku, Tokyo 160-0017, Japan.

CHAPTER–14

Spirituality in Action 24 x 7

Dr. Neerja Dhankar,
Principal,
Army Institute of Education

One of the noble, ultimate and highest aim of education is developing spirituality which remains unachieved through present day education which is preparing students for better economic pursuits only. There are frequent news of suicides by eminent prefessors and students of apex institutes of learning such as IITs and IIMs. Vocational aims are important but not at the cost of healthy physical, mental, social and spiritual life. Spirituality is not something which demands your time, energy and resources to perform any ritual. If we understand, it is part of daily life, very simple routine. It should be made into our habits. Let us see how.

- Get up early and immediately thank the Almighty for peaceful night and another good day ahead.
- Pure your body of all waste and lethargy, Cleanliness is Godliness.
- Watch Sun-rise and appreciate nature's beauty.
- Greet every member of family with smile and due respect according to age, traditions and customs.

- ❑ Have pure food and thank God for it and praise the person who prepared and served you.
- ❑ Leave home with an intention to be honest, sincere, dedicated to the profession, occupation, service you are into.
- ❑ Be courteous to every individual, or any living being on your way to work.
- ❑ Be punctual and regular for your job and your every role in the society.
- ❑ God resides with in every human being so do not insult / humiliate anyone anywhere. Even if you are in an authority position, remember to be modest. Remember, a lot had been accomplishedf before you were born. Thank God for your position and use your power for welfare of all who deserve.
- ❑ Try to meet deadlines without getting tense. There are peaceful means to get tasks accomplished successfully. Wise planning, continuous sincere efforts and perservance is the key to timely completion of every work successfully.
- ❑ Do not keep any negative emotions such as jealousy, auger, hatred in your heart for anyone. You should not be a store-house for negative emotions which may prevent positive energy to flow freely and enlighten you.
- ❑ Never use bad language for any one.
- ❑ Do not be afraid to accept failures, ask questions and be a constant learner. When you pray: pray for all as Almighty can provide every wish for everyone.
- ❑ Whatever you do; do with no ill will to anyone and with good for maximum. Do not do anything which you cannot do or accept in front of everyone. In short - Be true yourself. If not to anyone – you are accountable to self and God, as God in within you. It is very much part of you.
- ❑ Every movement, every place; look for people to whom you can be of some help.
- ❑ Love you critics, as they are the ones who tell you where you need improvement.

- ❑ Be a patient listener.
- ❑ Help others; you will find happiness in little acts of kindness.
- ❑ Have hobbies and interests and find time lto indulge in these. Be it poetry, painting, watching movies, gardening, social service or any other unique one.
- ❑ Spend quality time with your family members everyday and relatives and friends on regular basis. Do not wait to lose some dear ones to realize their importance later. Show love towards them when they are alive. Realise their importance before it is too late.
- ❑ Protect yourself from illness and weakness by naturopathy and yoga.
- ❑ Always remember death. That will keep your life on right track.
- ❑ Live simple life in thoughts, actions and behavious.
- ❑ Keep a pet if you can, give it proper care and quality time.
- ❑ Live life, do not just exist. Realise your potential; physical intellectual, spiritual, emotional and use it optionally for good of all.
- ❑ Be satisfied and peaceful soul always with whatever God has blessed you with. However do not stop working for betterment but do not be selfish greedy and dishonest to achieve anything in life.
- ❑ Be a constant learner. Life is a great teacher itself.
- ❑ Find opportunities to observe beauty of nature in big and small things such as smiles of children, sound of raindrops, songs of birds, sight of dew drops, eyes of various animals, shapes of trees, clouds, flowers on the grass and much more. Count you blessings not sorrows.
- ❑ Thanks God for sorrows too as these make you realize the importance of happiness and make you bold to face life's diversities. There are big lessons of life hidden behind sorrows. Accept your share gracefully. Do not complain.

- ❑ Do not forget to thank God for every before going for a peaceful night sleep.
- ❑ You can judge your goodness by imagingingping.

Who will cry,
When you die?

Practicing Spirituality is so simple. It does not need any rituals and sacrifices. Human beings are born spiritual. Do not let environment change your basic nature of goodness and spirituality.

If you are at peace with yourself, you are successful at being a spiritual person. So happy Go lucky, Practising Spirituality and spread it around in the environment as such things are caught and not taught.

Section-D

EXPANDING SPIRITUAL SPACE

CHAPTER–15

Thoughts of Eminent Indian Thinkers on Women's Education

Prof. Gouri Srivastava,
Head,
Department of Women's Studies, NCERT

Thoughts of eminent Indian thinkers is a reflection of the inner spirituality they had in their deep faith that women of India would contribute in any sphere given the opportunity. They had innate faith in the heart of humanity and penning their thoughts they envisioned the future role of womanhood in India. Few of these men and women questioned customary practices that would come in the way of spiritual advancement of women. Spirituality is when one has the innate courage to speak, voice opinion without fear and any kind of intimidation. It is the strength to work for the good of humanity so that compassion, sympathy and learning to live together is translated into practice.

The Indian cultural heritage has very rich examples of eminent persons like Raja Ram Mohan Roy, Ishwar Chand Vidyasagar, Swami Vivekananda, Dayanand Saraswati, Sri Aurobindo Ghosh, B.M. Malabari, Justice Ranade, Pandita Ramabai Saraswati, Ramabai

Ranade, Sarojini Naidu, Mahatma Gandhi, Jawaharlal Nehru and many more who have written about Indian women. Their various forms of literacy expositions depicted their immense faith in the women of India. In all their writings they linked social, economic and political progress of India with the improvement in the status of women. In their opinion involving half of the humanity would provide immense moral potential for sustaining India's freedom and independence. As a result of their inspirational thoughts parents were motivated to send their daughters to educational institutions. It is significant to note that in the mid 20th century some girls belonging to the social reformist families joined higher institutions of learning such as the S.N.D.T. University, the Bombay University and the Bethune College. Few women were also motivated to give up the customs and traditions that were derogatory to their status e.g. child marriage, purdah and enforced widowhood.

Several methods were initiated by reformers for bringing about a change in the social and educational status of women. The first method was to change the existing social structure by questioning the established customs and traditions adversely affecting women in a violent manner. Upholders of this school of thought believed that conscience after all must be the supreme guide of human conduct and therefore anything that impinged on the dignity of the human being had to be discarded. The second method was that of interpreting sacred text by justifying that the Vedic period was an era wherein women enjoyed a relatively better position. Followers of this method sought to bring about reformation by drawing parallels from earlier period and by interpreting sacred text, e.g. Raja Ram Mohan Roy was against the practice of sati that was widely prevalent in the Bengal Presidency. He tried to do away with this custom by stating neither the Vedas, nor Yajnavalkya supported it. In fact, it was forbidden both by the Bhagwad-Gita, Manu and Raghunanada; even the author of Mitakshara considered it inferior to eternal beauty or virtuous life. He further argued that even Harita and other advocates of sati did not support it if it was not voluntarily. Ishwar Chand Vidyasagar, the pioneer of widow remarriage stated that widow remarriage was sanctioned by the Shastras. The third was the method of pledges. The followers of this method appealed to men's sense of honour, irrespective of the opinions of society, the command of religious or personal convenience and comfort e.g. Maharshi Karve, the follower of this method pledged to marry a widow when his first wife expired. The fourth was the method of compromise. The follower of this school also believed in the necessity of reform although at the same time they were not themselves prepared, either from moral cowardice or because of the cumulative influence of tradition to act upon their honest belief, e.g. Gopal Hari Deshmukh, despite the vigour of his attack against the Brahmin priests, submitted to their demands that he go through a penance ceremony, including taking prayascitta for having attended the re-marriage of Hindu widow. The last or the fifth method laid emphasis on state compulsion, which in other words seeks to involve the assistance of the legislature. Many of the reformers, particularly Ishwar Chand Vidyasagar and Malabari encouraged the state to pass legislation on Widow Remarriage, Age of Consent and so on, as a result of which we find that Widow Remarriage Act was passed in 1856 and the Age of Consent Bill was passed in 1891, which raised the age of marriage of girls from ten to twelve.

Therefore, various methods were advocated by the reformers in bringing about a change in the existing social institutions. Despite, the methods being varied, there was a common underlying current, i.e. the desire of bringing change or reforms into the state of the society already in existence. Existing status quo was not accepted to them. Reformer's like Ranade did not believe in anyone of the prescribed stated methods, but believed in adapting any method that was required in a particular social context.

As a result of their thoughts and writing women were motivated to join the freedom struggle of India since its very inception. Just like their male counterpart they made powerful speeches in English and Vernaculars at different moments of the struggle and succeeded in mobilizing women folk from the urban and rural areas. In fact, they became role models for girls and women of their times. They also opened organizations like Sharda Sadan, Seva-Sadan, Vanita Vishram, the All India Women's Conference and many more. These organizations were spearheaded by woman who worked relentlessly for ameliorating the status of women by providing refuge to adults and child widows, destitute and girls from different socio-economic backgrounds. Social reformers and educated men and women of India, also made girls and women self-reliant by providing them education and practical training in vocations like sewing, knitting, tailoring and basket making etc.

It is note worthy to know that women who joined these organizations penned down their thoughts in the form of poetry, prose and other forms of literary expressions about their lived lives in the organizations that began during this period. In fact, their literary expressions got wide publicity in newspapers, journals and magazines of the said period. The sayings and thoughts of eminent thinkers of India are relevant even to this day for their inspirational messages which have the capacity of motivating parents from all walks of life to send their girl child to formal and non-formal schools.

In the context of education, there was a common consensus among the eminent thinkers that education would make women rational, aware and encourage them to think logically about the benefits of education in improving the overall quality of their own life and also of women folk in successive generations. It would in the long run convince them from submitting to customary practices and traditions that had a derogatory impact on their status. Further, educated women would themselves spearhead social, educational and political reforms that would help in creating a voice of the voiceless and help in generating women's perspective in all development activities.

In their speeches and writing, they suggested the following methods for educating girls belonging to different states –

- Opening formal educational institutions.
- Writing motivational literature for encouraging parents to send their daughters to formal institutions.
- Giving scholarships.
- Providing transport facilities.
- Appointing senior persons as escorts.

In the present paper, an attempt has been made to highlight the thoughts of some eminent men and women of India on education of girls and women.

Poet Dalpatram -

If one wants to improve society, one should give education to women. According to him, there were many advantages in educating one's daughter, even mentioning such things as the prevention of petty quarrels and petty obstacles among women. He added if a father gives dowry to his daughter, the husband would usurp it, if education is given to her no power on earth could deprive her of her wealth.

Source: Basu, Aparna, "A Century's Journey: Women's Education in Western India 1820-1920" in socialization education and women – Explorations in Gender Identity Ed. Karuna Chanana, N.M.M.L., New Delhi, 1988, p. 13.

Poet Narmada -

He urged the girls "to study, study and study". He argued that women should be educated as they were in no way inferior to men or their slaves......... By educating a woman, the man will benefit. An educated wife will help her husband, he will be able to talk to her and share his joys and sorrows...... An educated man cannot share his life with an illiterate wife. Education will make a woman a better wife, a better daughter-in-law and a better mother.

Source: Basu, Aparna, "A Century's Journey: Women's Education in Western India 1820-1920" in socialization education and women – Explorations in Gender Identity Ed. Karuna Chanana, N.M.M.L., New Delhi, 1988, p. 13.

Sri Aurobindo –

The education of a human being should begin at birth and continue throughout his life. Indeed, if we want this education to have its maximum result, it should begin even before birth; in this case it is the mother herself who proceeds with this education by means of a manifold action; first, upon herself for her own improvement, and secondly, upon the child whom she is forming physically. For it is certain that the nature of the child to be born depends very much upon the mother who forms it, upon her aspiration and will as well as upon the material surroundings in which she lives. To see that her thoughts are always beautiful and pure, her feelings always noble and fine, her material surroundings as harmonious as possible and full of a great simplicity – this is the part of education which should apply to the mother herself. And if she has in addition a conscious and definite will to form the child according to the highest ideal she can conceive, then the very best conditions will be realized so that the child can come into the world with his utmost potentialities. How many difficult efforts and useless complications would be avoided in this way. Education to be complete must have five principal aspects corresponding to the five principal activities of the human being: the physical, the vital, the mental, the psychic and spiritual. Usually, these phases of education follow chronologically the growth of the individual; this however, does not mean that one of them should replace another, but that all must continue, completing one another until the end of his life.....

Source: On Women: Compiled from the writings of Sri Aurobindo and the Mother, p. 34.

Annie Besant –

And here we must repeat our often reiterated declaration that the education of Indian girls must be shaped, guided and controlled by Indians, else will the heart of the Nation be corrupted and the motherland, which ahs survived all wounds to her men, will perish by the despiritualization and the denationalization of her women. The religion of Indian women is often not according to knowledge; perfect in her devotion, she is lacking in philosophical insight: of swift intelligence and quick intuition she grasps with ease a great truth when it is presented to her, and sees its application to life; but she if often taught but forms and ceremonies, which she uses as channels for her devotion without rationalizing them by her understanding 'Add to you faith, knowledge', is a percept needed in the home. Whatever else woman's education may comprise, Hinduism, spiritual and lofty, must be its foundation and its coping-stone; when Hinduism has no longer its temple in the heart of the Hindu woman, the motherland will be ready for the burning-ghat.

The ethics taught in the education of girls must include patriotism the realization of duty to the motherland, of readiness to sacrifice for her weal Indian history, is full of the shining examples of such love and such sacrifice, and the stories of these daughters, of the motherland will give what is needed.

Apart from every other reason the necessity for religious and moral education is sufficient basis for the statement that the education of Indian girls must be under Indian control... Indian history, Indian scripture, Indian dramas, Indian arts – these must dominate the education of Indian girls.

Source: Grover, Verinder and Arora Ranjana, 'Great Women of Modern India', Deep and Deep Publication, p. 119.

Annie Besant –

For any education beyond the most elementary, it is obvious that pre-puberty marriage must be abolished. Children married at 7, 9 and 10, at 11 and 12, how can they be educated? Made mothers at 13 and 14, children bearing children, of what avail to mention education in the same breath as these?

Ibid, p. 120

Sister Nivedita –

The question that has to be solved for Indian women, therefore, is a form of education and might attain this end of, developing the faculties of soul and mind in harmony with one another.

Source: Grover, Verinder and Arora Ranjana, 'Great Women of Modern India', Deep and Deep Publication, 1993, p. 224.

Dhondo Keshav Karve –

The best way to advance the cause was, I thought, to educate widows. Education would make them self-supporting and would enable them to think for themselves parents and guardian of widows look more to self-interest rather than the interest of their wards and avoid humiliation and molestation from society widows, when education, would understand their own interests and if able to muster sufficient courage, would be ready for a practical step. The Hindu Widow's Home Association was formally established on 14th June 1896 with Dr. R.G. Bhandarkar as President.

Source: Dhondo Keshav Karve, "Looking Back", p. 59.

Parvatibai Athavale-

It was the education I received that made questions revolve in my mind, as to the real meaning of the country of India, her natural life and what is needed to be done for the national uplift.

Source: Dev. Abbott, E. Justin, (translated). Hindu Widow: An Autobiography by Mrs. Parvatibai Athavale.

Parvatibai Athavale-

Education awakened my mind. I determined on carrying out my ideal. And for this purpose I decided to give my whole life to the service of the widows' home. To help Professor Karve in his work I went to Hingane to live, and set myself directly to work.

Ibid, p. 30

Nawab Sultan Jahan Begum –

Education to my mind is the best ornament of a woman. It is perhaps forgotten that women, too, are half the community and no real progress can be achieved if the educational needs to this important area neglected and starved of.

In her mind, she was having an appropriate curriculum for female education and in this reference she further writes at one place of her account: "In my opinion, imperfect education is worse than none at all. The sweet water of this spring should either be drunk deep or not tasted at all. It is a stupid thing to my mind, to teach the girls to read and write, and then leave them to their fate. The very least that should be done for them, is to give them a thorough grounding in things that matter, and to awaken the dormant soul in them.

Source: Quoted from Begum, H.H. Nawab Sultan Jahan, An Account of My Life, Vol. II, translated by Major Abdus Samad Khan, Bombay, 1922.

Nawab Sultan Jahan Begum –

Culture is the basis of civilization, and female education is the key to culture...... and now, my daughters, let me ask you to make the most of the opportunities that have been given too you seek diligently to acquire knowledge, which is a woman's wealth, and culture, which is her adornment; but do not forget that true comeliness consists in nobility of character. In this way you will grow up to be loved by old and young; - misfortunes will be unable to crush you, and worldly prosperity will never make you proud. Remember that the object of your education is not that you may undertake that duties of me; but that you may acquire those womanly accomplishments and virtues which will enable you to become capable housewives and good mothers. The management of a home and the training of a child are two of the noblest and most responsible of human duties, and God created woman for their performance.

Source: Quoted from Begum, H.H. Nawab Sultan Jahan, An Account of My Life, Vol. II, translated by C.H. Payne, Bombay, 1927 Mittal, Kamla. Op. cit. 1901-1949", p. 89.

Mahatma Gandhi –

Education according to Gandhiji was necessary evil so far as women were concerned. It would not only enlighten them but make them aware of their present circumstances and prevalent customs and traditions. Perhaps it would motivate them and prevent them from succumbing to it. It would also sharpen their intellect. In other words he felt that be it man or woman, a person without education is akin to animal.

A woman is the companion of man gifted with equal mental capacities. She has the right to participate in very minutest details in the activities of man and she has an equal right of freedom and liberty within.

Source: Mehta, Hansa. "Indian Women", Butala and Company, Baroda, 1981.

Aruna Asaf Ali –

It is widely known that before independence, during the days of British rule, arrangements for the education of the masses being practically non-exist, orthodoxy and dogmatism flourished and people, particularly women, remained steeped in poverty and ignorance, shackled to tradition, customs and age-old superstitions. But the wheels of change had started revolving from the later years of the 19th century. And several illustrious men and women pioneered the social reform movement in many parts of our country.

Source: Grover, Verinder and Arora, Ranjana, Great Women of Modern India, Deep and Deep Publication, New Delhi, 1993, p. 68.

Durgabai Deshmukh-

Economic growth means not only creation of wealth but also creating people's capacity to create wealth and that resides in their health, education, knowledge, skills etc. It is very difficult to separate the two social welfare has to be society's organized expression of concern for the total well being of its members. It is not some temporary relief measure but consists of long term rehabilitation.

Source: Annual Report 2001-2002, Department of Women and Child Development, MHRD, Government of India, p. 175.

Proceedings of Indian Social Reformer –

Women's education therefore is the pivot round which the whole question of social religious and domestic reform hangs, ... The home and the family is the social unit and forms the centre or the heart of the body which the life blood is circulated to the whole organism of society. Women then form an essential part of the system and an important factor too is as much as the stamp to the character of the future generation is given by her e.g. her conduct.

Source: Indian Social Reformer, p. 386.

Jawaharlal Nehru-

For the women of India, for all their charm and intelligence and capacity for good work, have been too long neglected. I believe that India has a great future, but I also believe that real and rapid progress in India will only come when our womenfolk get really moving and rid themselves of everything that suppresses them and keeps them back. Because I see clear and definite signs of the movement. I am full of hope for India, and because our national movement has been largely instrumental in releasing women from many an old bond, that movement has demonstrated its essential soundness and vitality.

Source: From forward to Rajkumari Amrit Kaur's Challenge to Women, 7 March, 1946.

Jawaharlal Nehru-

Truly no argument is required in defence of women's education. For my part, I have always been strongly of the opinion that while it may be possible to neglect men's education it is not possible or desirable to neglect women's education.

The reasons are obvious. If you educate the women, probably men will also be affected thereby, and in any event children will be affected. For every educationist knows that the formative years of a person's life are the first seven or eight years. We talk about schools, and colleges which are not doubt important, but a person is more or less made in the first ten years of his or her life. Obviously, in that period, it is the mother who counts most of all.

Therefore the mother who has been well trained in various ways becomes essential to education. Most mothers, trained otherwise, I regret to say, are not good mothers.

The idea that women should be kept away from most occupations no longer finds favour. It might be that certain occupations are not suited for women but that is a different matter. There are plenty of occupations which they could engage in and which they do engage in. If we analyse the matter carefully, we shall find that the average woman in India works in the field. In fact both man and woman work in the field. It is only when one gets to the middle class that the question of distinction arises. The great majority of our women have to work because economic circumstances compel them to work. Unfortunately, the idea has been prevailing – I am glad to see that it is rapidly fading – that the less work one does the higher is one's status in society.

Whatever group or religion one might belong to, education is essential. By education I mean education and not merely learning to be ladylike. Learning to be lady-like may be good in itself but it is not education as such.

Education has mainly two aspects, the cultural aspect which makes a person grow, and the productive aspect which makes a person do things. Both are essential. Everybody should be a producer as well as a good citizen and not a sponge on another person even though the other person may be one's own husband or wife. That is the way we are developing and persons who do not wake up to this fact and prepare themselves for it will just be left behind. So it is highly necessary that we should develop our education, among our girls more especially, because men are provided for to some extent. There are still inhibitions in the case of Muslim girls' education and these should be removed, because, apart from any other big reason, common sense tell us do.

Source: From the speech at the foundation of a women's college, in Madras, 22 January, 1955.

Rabindranath Tagore-

O Lord, why have you not given woman the right to conquer her destiny? Why does she have to wait head bowed? By the roadside, waiting with tired patience, hoping for a miracle in the morrow.

Source: Annual Report, 2002-2003, Department of Women and Child Development, MHRD, New Delhi.

Folk song from Madhya Pradesh-

We sing of our pain and suffering, we have bad dreams – no one understands. One day our life will be different. A new sun is about to rise. A new future awaits us.

Source: Annual Report, 2002-2003, Department of Women and Child Development, MHRD, New Delhi.

Sarojini Naidu-

The word education is the most misunderstood word in any language... The instruction being merely the accumulation of knowledge, might indeed, lend itself to conventional definition, but education is an immeasurable, beautiful, indispensable atmosphere in which we live and move and have our being. Does one man dare to deprive another of his birthright to God's pure air which nourishes his body? …….. How then shall a man dare to deprive a human soul of its immemorial inheritance of liberty and life? Your fathers, in depriving your mother of that immemorial birthright have robbed you, their sons, of your just inheritance. Therefore, I charge you, restore to your women their ancient rights, for, as I have said, it is we, and not you, who are the real national builders, and without our active co-operation at all points of progress all your Congresses and Conferences are in vain. Educate your women and the nation will take care of itself, for it is as true today as it was yesterday and will be to the end of human life that the hand that rocks the cradle rules the world.

Source: Radha Kumar, The History of Doing: An Illustrated Account of Movements for Women's Rights and Feminism in India, 1800-1900, p. 50

Sarojini Naidu-

It seems to me a paradox, at once touched with humour and tragedy, than on the very threshold of the twentieth century, it should still be necessary for us to stand upon public platform and pass resolutions in favour of what is called female education in India- in all places in India, which, at the beginning of the first century was already ripe with civilization and had contributed to the world's progress radiant examples of women of the highest genius and wildest culture. But as by some irony of evolution of evolution the paradox stands to our shame, it is time for us to consider how best we can remove such a reproach, how we can best achieve something more fruitful than the passing of empty resolutions in favour of female education from year to year. At this great moment of stress and striving, when the Indian races are seeking for the ultimate unity of a common national ideal, it is well for us to remember that the success of the whole movement lies centered in what is known as the woman question. It is not you but we who are the true nation builders…..

Source: Speeches and writings of Sarojini Naidu, G.A. Natesan and Co., Madras.

Conclusion

Thus, 19th and 20th centuries was an era of great men and women of India who were keenly interested in promoting social and educational status of women from all walks of life. They worked relentlessly by opening schools for girls, provided financial assistance, wrote literary expositions on importance of girls' education in different print media for motivating and making community aware that educating half of the humanity was a pre-condition for social and economic development of the country. They firmly believed that if women were convinced about the value of education successive generation would automatically benefit from education. Eminent thinkers never envisaged immediate social change as they were realistic and aware that this issue would take a long gestation time. In an age wherein there existed entrenched notional believe that educating girls would lead to early widowhood, make girls defiant and a firm believe among different communities that household chores needed no formal guidance would take a long time for convincing people about educating their daughters. This would perhaps require sustained efforts on a long term basis.

The kind of education that eminent Indian thinkers propagated related to the roles women were already performing in their private sphere. The focus was on improving the quality of life of family and the multifaceted roles that women were already performing. Few women who benefited from education in the said period also took to professions like teaching, nursing, mid-wife, doctors and as social reformers. Some of them like Pandita Ramabai Saraswati and Ramabai Ranade opened organizations that looked into the education and self-reliance of girls from poor background. The thoughts of eminent Indian thinkers are relevant and continued to inspire parents and communities for promoting education and empowerment of girls.

References

Abbott, E. Justin (1986) *Hindu Widow,* an Autobiography by Mrs. Pravati Athavale, New Delhi.

Annual Report (2002-2003) Department of Women and Child Development, MHRD, New Delhi.

Basu, Aparna (1988) *A Century's Journey: Women's Education in Western India 1820-1920,* in Socialization Education and Women-explorations in Gender Identity, Ed. Karuna Chanana, N.M.M.L. New Delhi.

Basu, Aparna (1984) *Gujarati Women's Response to Gandhi 1920-42,* Samya Shakti, A Journal of Women's Studies, Vol. 7, No. 2, Centre for Women's Development Studies, New Delhi.

Dua, Asha (2003) *Qhotes by Indian Women,* Ikon Publishers, New Delhi.

Gandhi, M.K. (1935) *Young India, 1927-1928,* Madras.

Gidumal, Dayaram (1888) *The Life and Life Work of Behramjji,* Mr. Malabari, Bombay.

Grover, Verinder and Arora, Ranjana (1993) *Great Women of Modern India,* Deep and Deep Publications, New Delhi.

Jawaharlal Nehru's Thoughts on Women (1989) Women and Child Development, New Delhi.

Kamla, Mittal (1990) *History of Bhopal State: Development of Constitution, Administration and national Awakening 1901-1949,* Munshiram Manoharlal Publishers, Delhi.

Karve, D.K. (1936) *Looking Back,* Poona.

Kumar, Radha (1993) *The History of Doing: An Illustrated Account of Movements for Women's Rights and Feminism in India 1800-1900,* Kali for Women, New Delhi.

Mehta, Hansa (1981) *Indian Women,* Butala and Company, Baroda.

Minault, Gali (1999) *Secluded Scholars: Women's Education and Muslim Social Reform in Colonial India,* Oxford University Press.

Natarajan, K. (1890) *The Indian Social Reformer,* Weekly.

Natesam, G.A., *Speeches and Writings of Sarojini Naidu,* G.A. Natesam & Col., Madras.

Srivastava, Gouri (2000) *Women's Higher Education in the 19th Century,* Concept Publishing Company, New Delhi.

Sultan Jahan Begum (1922) *Taj-ul-Ikbal Traik Bhopal,* or the History of Bhopal, Trans. H.C. Barstow, Calcutta.

Vijay (2007) *On Women Compiled from the Writings of Sri Aurobindo and the Mother,* Sri Aurobindo Society, New Delhi.

CHAPTER–16

MAHATMA GANDHI & *THE BHAGAVAD GITA*

Dr. Y.P. Anand,
Former Chairman, Railway Board, & Director,
National Gandhi Museum, New Delhi

Mohandas Karamchand Gandhi, revered universally as Mahatma Gandhi, remained deeply and continuously absorbed in public and political life, in South Africa and then in India, from 1893 till his martyrdom on January 30, 1948. However, even before 1893, he had become acquainted with the *Bhagavad Gita* during his student days in London. His study of the *Gita* too grew and deepened along with his involvement in public and national struggles. By the time he returned to India in 1915 from South Africa, he was already living his life according to the tenets of the *Gita* and had taken to it as his primary source of ethical, moral and spiritual inspiration. No wonder, he applied its teachings widely in the political, social and economic fields during his stewardship of India's freedom struggle.

Gandhiji writes in his *Autobiography* that his father, in his last days, "began reading the *Gita* at the instance of a learned Brahmin friend of the family - -." He himself had no knowledge of the *Gita* till "towards the end of my second year in England." Thus it was in 1890 at about 21 years of age that he came across two Theosophist brothers who invited him to read the *Gita* in original with them. He told them that he had not read it in Sanskrit or in Gujarati till then, but though his knowledge of Sanskrit was meager, still he hoped to understand the original "to the extent of telling them when the translation failed to bring out the meaning." He started reading Sir Edwin Arnold's translation of the *Gita, The Song Celestial*, with them. However, he could not "pretend to have studied it then." It "was only after some years that it became a book of daily reading." Yet the verses 62 and 63 of Chapter II "made a deep impression on my mind and they still ring in my ears." Further, "The book struck me as one of priceless worth. The impression has been ever since growing on me that I regard it today [1927] as the book *par excellence* for the knowledge of truth. It has afforded me invaluable help in my moments of gloom. I have read almost all the English translations of it, and I regard Sir Edwin Arnold's as the best."

After his return to India from England in 1891, he found in a young Jain, Raychandbhai, his spiritual guide. He arrived in South Africa in 1893, and has recorded in his Diary [1894]: "Received a long letter from Brother discussing *Gita*." In South Africa, he went through a period of deep religious fermentation and read Christian, Hindu and Muslim scriptures. In his quest for rediscovering his own Hindu *dharma*, he sent a list of 27 questions to Raychandbhai for elucidation. Of these Q.10 was: "Who is the author of the *Gita*? Is God its author? Is there any evidence that He is?" With the issue of the authorship of the *Gita* thus got clarified, henceforth he was concerned fully with its teachings and their application in life. He wrote in his *Autobiography*: "I already had faith in the *Gita* - -. Now I realized the necessity of diving deeper into it. - - I decided also to get by heart one or two verses every day. - - - I employed the time of my morning ablutions. - - - This time was found sufficient for memorizing - - the thirteen chapters. But the memorizing - - had to give way to - - *satyagraha* - - but to me the *Gita* became an infallible guide of conduct - - my dictionary of daily reference - - a ready solution of all my troubles and trials. Words like *aparigraha* [non-possession] and *samabhava* [*samatava*: equable attitude toward all] gripped me."

He called the *Gita* as 'Mother', 'the Book of life', and his 'refuge'. He declared that his "life is based on the teachings of the *Gita.*" To him, the *Gita* "answers all my difficulties and has been my *Kamadhenu*, the Cow of plenty, my guide, my open sesame, at hundreds of moments of doubt and difficulty. I cannot recall a single occasion when it has failed me". It is "our spiritual dictionary", "the only dictionary of reference, in which I find all the sorrows, all the troubles, all the trials arranged in the alphabetical order with the exquisite solutions", "the divine poem", and "the key to a knowledge of the *Shastras.* It enunciates the principles on which all conduct must be based." He said that, "The *Gita* is the living, life-giving immortal mother. - - - No Hindu should remain ignorant of it." "It simply describes the progress of the pilgrim soul towards the Supreme Goal." It was "all-sufficing for me, because it not only conforms to the first principles, but gives you reasons for adherence to them at any cost."

While the *Gita* served as his friend, philosopher and guide in practically all matters, public and personal, he also extensively wrote and spoke on the various aspects and the teachings of the *Gita.* He has, in fact, given very comprehensive and contemporary, even revolutionary meanings and interpretation of the numerous aspects of its teaching, doctrine and philosophy. He applied his usual uncanny approach to go to the heart of the matter and state his understanding of the *Gita* and its various verses, in a language at once simple and profound. Without being a lSanskrit scholar of high order, yet he qualifies to be considered as the most recent *bhashyakar* (interpreter, analyzer) of the *Gita*, in the illustrious line starting with Adi Shakracharya and Ramanuja and going up to Tilak and Sri Aurobindo in modern times.

It is commonly not known that Mahatma Gandhi has probably written more 'Works' on the *Gita* than any other *Bhashyakar* (interpreter). While in Yervada jail in 1923, he compiled a dictionary of all the words in the *Gita* with their meanings in Gujarati, which was published in 1936 under the title '*Gitapadarthakosha*'. Then during 1926, in the Satyagraha Ashram, Sabarmati, he delivered 218 discourses in Gujarati on the *Gita*. These have been composed and published under the title '*Gitashikshan*'. Thereafter he translated, into Gujarati, each verse of the *Gita* and, along with his 'Introduction'– one of the finest summations of the philosophy of the *Gita* ever written–, and it was published under the title '*Anasaktiyoga*' [later translated into English by Mahadev Desai under the title, 'The Gospel of Selfless Action, or, The *Gita* According to Gandhi] on March 12, 1930, the day he started his historic 'Salt March' from the Satyagraha Ashram, Ahmedabad. Again, during 1931 and 1932, while in jail, he sent, through weekly letters, his written 'discourses' – one on each chapter of the *Gita* – for the benefit of the *ashramites* who had found even the '*Anasaktiyoga*' difficult to comprehend. These were published under the title '*Gitabodh*'.

Apart from these four major 'Works' by Mahatma Gandhi on the *Bhagavad Gita*, there are hundreds of his articles, letters and speeches or interviews in which he refers to it and its teachings in the context of nearly every conceivable subject, context and situation. These, designated by me as 'Miscellaneous References', in fact, constitute the core of his interpretation of the *Gita* and its application as the 'dictionary' of human life in all its aspects.

For any deep study of Mahatma Gandhi's life and thought, it is essential to understand his lifelong *engagement* with the 'Mother *Gita*'. With this humble objective I have compiled/ written the book, "Mahatma Gandhi's 'Works' & Interpretation of the *Bhagavad Gita*" (published in two volumes in 2009) in order to present Gandhiji's various 'Works', the 'Miscellaneous References', and his understanding of the *Gita* together in one place as a work of reference for the students, scholars and seekers of Gandhian thought and of the *Bhagavad Gita*.

Gandhiji had truly made the *Gita* a people's scripture and guide to life. It no more remained an exclusive preserve of the scholars, *acharyas, bhashyakars,*or religious preachers. Like the 'Mother Ganges' was brought down to the earth by Bhagirath, 'Mother *Gita*' has been 'brought down' by Gandhiji as a precious treasure within an easy reach of every person. This he has achieved by his relating the understanding and application of its teachings to nearly every activity of human existence. Whenever in difficulty, in doubt, in depression, or in disappointment, he would dip into the inexhaustible ready wisdom of "the living life-giving immortal mother", the *Gita,* and find the necessary answer, solace and guidance. And, as advised by him to his friends and co-workers, so can anyone else. We have only to dive deep into it following the sure lead of Mahatma Gandhi.

We need learned and competent persons to take the task forward and write ever more discerning treatises in various languages on Gandhiji's 'Works' and understanding of the *Gita.* He believed in the dynamic evolution of the interpretation of scriptures like the *Gita,* so that it remains relevant to the needs of the changing character of human society. This approach must inform the study of the *Gita* in order to avoid pitfalls of dogmatism and irrelevance.

Gandhiji himself has given an excellent summary of his interpretation of the *Gita* in the 'Introduction' ('Message of the *Gita*) to his translation of the *Gita* into Gujarati, titled '*Anasaktiyoga*'. He had himself translated the 'Introduction' into English, this translation first appearing in *Young India* on August 6, 1931. [vide *The Collected Works of Mahatma Gandhi,* vol. 41, p.90-101] Selected references/ extracts from his 'Introduction' to the '*Anasaktiyoga*' are given below in order to present an outline of his interpretation of the *Gita*:

- The *Gita* is not a historical work, but under the guise of physical warfare, it describes the duel between good and evil that perpetually goes on in the heart of every human being.
- "The author of the *Mahabharata* has not established the necessity of physical warfare; on the contrary he has proved its futility. - -

made the victors shed tears of sorrow and repentance. - -. In the characteristics of the perfected man of the *Gita* [chapter II], I do not see any to correspond to physical warfare."

- "Krishna of the *Gita* is perfection and right knowledge personified; but the picture is imaginary. - - In Hinduism, incarnation is ascribed to one who has performed some extraordinary service of mankind. - - Krishna enjoys, in Hinduism, the status of the most perfect incarnation."
- "Man is not at peace with himself till he has become like unto God. - - - And this is self-realization. - - The object of the *Gita* appears to me to be that of showing the most excellent way to attain self-realization. - - *That Matchless Remedy is Renunciation of Fruits of Action.*"
- "There must be action where there is body. - - Every action is tainted, - - how can one be free from - - the taint of sin? - - - 'By desireless action, by renouncing fruits of action; by dedicating all activities to God - -.' But - - Right knowledge is necessary for attaining renunciation - - In order that knowledge may not run riot, the author of the *Gita* has insisted on devotion accompanying it and has given it the first place. - - *Gita's* assessment of the devotee's qualities is similar to that of the sage's. - - the devotion required by the *Gita* is - - not blind faith - - has the least to do with externals. - - to be a real devotee is to realize oneself. - - if the means and the end are not identical, they are almost so. The extreme of means is salvation. - - But renunciation of fruit is no way means indifference to the result. - - Renunciation means absence of hankering after fruit."
- "- - the *Gita* - - has drawn no line of demarcation between salvation and worldly pursuits. On the contrary - - religion must rule even our worldly pursuits. - - Thus, all acts that are incapable of being performed without attachment are taboo."
- If one tries "to enforce in one's life the central teaching of the *Gita*, one is bound to follow Truth and *ahimsa* [non-violence]. When there is no desire for fruit, there is no temptation for untruth or *himsa* [violence]. - - But it may be freely admitted

that the *Gita* was not written to establish *ahimsa*. - - The *Gita* had to deliver the message of renunciation of fruit."

- The meaning of important words evolves like human society itself. It is in this sense that the word *Yajna* ('sacrifice') in the *Gita* does not denote animal sacrifice at all, but "continuous concentration on God is the king of sacrifices". In chapter III "sacrifice chiefly means body-labour for service", and there are other meanings in chapters III and IV. Similarly, "The *Sanayasa* of the *Gita* will not tolerate complete cessation of all activity." It is "all work and yet no work."
- The *Gita* is "meant for the people at large - - With every age the important words will carry new and expanding meanings. But its central teaching will never vary. The seeker is at liberty to extract from this treasure any meaning he likes so as to enable him to enforce in his life the central teaching. - - - Desirelessness [*Anasakti*] is obligatory."
- The *Gita's* Knowledge is "beyond the mere intellect; it is essentially addressed to the heart - -. Therefore the *Gita* is not for those who have no faith."

Mahatma Gandhi made the *Gita* the scriptural guide of life's total conduct for himself as well as for everyone else. He interpreted the *Gita* for the masses, duly laying down its all-encompassing tapestry of the various paths towards self-realisation, the critical path of selfless service, duty and action as the core of its teaching — *Anasaktiyoga* (the *Yoga* of detached action), and the guidelines to human conduct as laid down in the *Gita* for a *Sthitprajna* (a person of steady wisdom), a *Bhakta* (a devotee), a *Jnani* (one who has knowledge), a *Trigunatita* (who has attained a state beyond the three *Gunas*), a *Daivasampadvan* (one who has divine qualities), and a *Brahamabhuta* (who has achieved the state of Brahman). The qualities of conduct indicated in each case are broadly similar and complimentary.

To Gandhiji, the *Gita* was the all-sufficing Mother and anyone who has faith and follows the precept of Action without desire for fruit [*Anasakti-Karma-Yoga*], can take refuge in its bosom. This interpretation of the *Gita*, is completely in tune with the life that Gandhiji himself led, towards the end of which he could say, "My life is my message". That is the message of the *Gita* as lived by him.

CHAPTER-17

INTEGRATING SPIRITUALITY AND PSYCHOTHERAPY

Amita Puri,
Army Inst. of Education

Introduction

Professional and scientific psychology appears to have rediscovered spirituality and religion during recent years (e.g., Hartz, 2005; McMinn & Dominquez, 2005; Plante & Sherman, 2001). There have been a large number of conferences, seminars, workshops, books, and special issues in major professional journals on spirituality and psychology integration of late.

Curiously, while a number of our prominent psychology forefathers such as William James, Carl Jung, and Gordon Allport were keenly interested in the relationship between psychology and religion (e.g., Allport, 1950; Jung, 1938), most of professional and scientific psychology during the past century has avoided the connection between these two areas of inquiry. For example, Collins (1977) stated: " . . . *psychology has never shown much interest in religion*

. . . apart from a few classic studies . . . the topic of religious behavior has been largely ignored by psychological writers" (p. 95).

Perhaps psychologists have been overly influenced by the words and perspectives of leaders in the field such as Sigmund Freud, B. F. Skinner, John Watson, and Albert Ellis who found little, if any, value in the study or practice of religion. For example, in *Future of an Illusion,* Freud (1927/1961) stated that religious views "are illusions, fulfillments of the oldest, strongest and most urgent wishes of mankind" (p. 30) and referred to religion as an "*obsessional neurosis*" (p. 43). Psychology has had a long history of being neglectful, if not outright antagonistic, to issues related to spirituality and religion, often finding those who are spiritual or religious as being deluded or at least not as psychologically healthy and advanced as they could be (e.g., Ellis, 1971; Freud, 1927/1961). While Freud called religious interests "*neurotic*" (p. 43), Watson (1924/1983) referred to religion as a "*bulwark of medievalism*" (p. 1).

Furthermore, psychology in the 20th century prided itself on being a serious science and perhaps tended to shy away from all things religious or spiritual in an effort to maximize and emphasize the rigorous scientific approach to both research and clinical practice. Since much of religion and spirituality concerns matters that were not readily observable or measurable, the field tended to stay as far away as possible from religious and spiritual constructs in an effort to prove that psychology should be taken seriously as a rigorous, empirical, and respected discipline (Ellis, 1971; Richards & Bergin, 1997; Watson, 1924/1983). Those psychologists who were religious or spiritual and wanted to integrate their faith traditions into their professional work generally needed to keep their interests fairly quiet and certainly would not profess their beliefs during the more vulnerable years of graduate and postgraduate training.

Researching, not patholising spirituality

Toward the very end of the 20th century, psychology (as well as science in general) has embraced spirituality and religion more and has used rigorous scientific methods such as double-blind randomized clinical trials to examine important questions related to psychology and religion integration (Miller, 1999; Miller & Thoresen, 2003; Plante & Sherman, 2001). These include the influence of religious and spiritual behaviors and beliefs on both mental and physical health outcomes (Koenig, McCullough, & Larson, 2001; Pargament, 1997; Plante & Sharma, 2001). Perhaps this is due to the increasing interest among the general population and psychotherapy clients in spirituality and health integration as well as the increasing media attention to this topic.

Taken together, most of the quality research in this area supports the connection between faith and health (Koening et al., 2001; Pargament, 1997; Plante & Sherman, 2001; Richards & Bergin, 1997). Furthermore, since the vast majority of people around the world consider themselves to be spiritual and/or religious (Gallup, 2006; Myers, 2000), many have been demanding that health professionals (including mental health professionals) **respect, acknowledge, and integrate** spirituality and religious principles into their professional work (Miller, 1999). Psychology's new focus on "***positive psychology***" also underscores the desire for a more friendly relationship between religion and psychology (Verma 2006). While both research and practice now support benefit to the integration of psychology and religion, some critics have cautioned that the integration of religion and spirituality into psychology and science is ethically, professionally, and scientifically dangerous (Sloan, 1999, 2001).

Curiously, during recent years many mental health professionals, including psychologists, have become interested in spirituality and religion as part of their professional work and are seeking ways to better integrate spirituality into their psychotherapy activities (Miller, 1999; O'Hanlon, 2006). Yet, almost all graduate and postgraduate training programs still offer no training in this integration (American Psychological Association, 2006; Russell & Yarhouse, 2006).

Too often in the past, highly religious or spiritually minded persons usually were pathologized by professional psychology and individual clinicians. They were often considered defended, insecure, deluded, and thought to be suffering from some important psychological dysfunction needing treatment (e.g., Ellis, 1971; Freud, 1927/1961). Their views and beliefs were certainly not respected. The 2002 APA Ethics Code and other professional ethics codes now articulate the need to respect the beliefs and values associated with religion and spirituality and to avoid pathologizing those who seek religious and spiritual growth, development, and involvement. While we are not required to agree with all faith beliefs and faith-based behaviors and even might find some religious points of view distasteful and destructive to health and well-being, we are asked to be respectful of the religious and spiritual beliefs, behaviors, and traditions of others.

The question of Competency

Since the vast majority of graduate and postgraduate training programs currently ignore spirituality and religious integration in professional training, how can mental health professional competently provide the much-needed services of integration? Clearly, professionals are on their own to get adequate training and supervision to ensure that they provide state-of-the-art and competent professional services if they plan to integrate spirituality and religion into their professional psychological work. Luckily, today there are many quality workshops, conferences, seminars, books, articles, and even special series of professional journals dedicated to religion and spirituality integration in psychology.

Furthermore, securing ongoing professional consultation with experts in integration is now likely possible in many locations due to the popularity of the topic. Psychologists and other mental health professionals need to be keenly aware of their areas of competence and not overstep their limits and skills.

Some therapeutic concerns

According to systems-oriented family therapy, one of the principal sources of distress in families is the failure of its members to communicate directly with each other. Anxious over the possible consequences of honest disclosure, they will confide in substitutes—other family members, lovers, and friends––rather than communicating with the ones with whom they have difficulties (Bowen, 1978; Hoffman, 1981). This proclivity for avoiding direct communication by turning to surrogates was first acknowledged by Bowen who, in believing that dyadic relationships are inherently unstable, came to regard triangles as "the smallest stable relationship structure" and triangulation as a problematic dynamic in families (Bowen, 1978). Trained as a psychoanalyst, Bowen recast Freud's original conception of the Oedipal triangle into a here-and-now emotional process that can take place between any three people.

Fogarty (1976) contributed to the concept by approaching triangles in treatment planning more structurally by moving distanced parents closer to their children, or by creating more distance between overinvolved parents and their children. Guerin went on to differentiate between "triangulation" as the reactive emotional process that activates a triangle, and a "triangle" as a relationship structure (Guerin, Fogarty, Fay, & Kautto, 1996). Minuchin further developed the idea by describing how a triangle could express itself as a "cross-generational coalition" between one parent and a child against the other parent, or as "detouring" in which parents channel their relationship distress onto a child (1974).

If the anxious avoidance of direct communication promotes triangulation, then encouraging honest communication, in which the individuals take responsibility for their respective contributions to the relationship, constitutes a priority in alleviating marital and family distress. Bowen believed that the best way to assist in "detriangling" was to remain neutral and to ask questions designed to help the conflicted family members become more aware of their respective contributions to the problem and what they needed to change in their own behavior in order to facilitate improvement in the relationship. In so doing, Bowen (1978) believed that a therapist could participate in a "therapeutic triangle," which instead of serving as a substitute for honest communication, creates a transitional context in which distressed family members can deal openly with their differences through the mediation of a respectful witness.

Triangles in Sacred Traditions

One does not have to look very far to discover triangles and triangulation functioning in the spiritual life. In religion traditions where the divine is considered ontologically distinct from the human realm—such as in Judaism, and in post-Augustinian Western Christianity—the gulf between heaven and earth constitutes an a priori condition that confronts every human being. This division is not a problem that can be resolved simply through a change in perspective, or a breakthrough in awareness. However, in other traditions, such as in Hinduism and Buddhism, God or higher consciousness is considered humankind's essential nature and ultimate destiny. Human beings are estranged from higher power not ontologically, but psychologically—that is, through a lack of awareness of their true selves. As one might expect, triangles in the Judeo-Christian tradition tend to become enshrined as permanent and necessary aspects of one's relationship with God, whereas triangles in Hinduism and Buddhism are, at least in principle, symbolic and transitional.

Progressive Triangles in the Eastern Tradition

In Buddhism and Hinduism, the problem of humanity's separation from higher power is psychological—or a matter of perception or awareness—rather than theological (Suzuki, 1987). According to these religions, human beings labor under the illusion, not the fact, of their estrangement from God. The resolution of humanity's perceived estrangement is always available through a complete release from the conditioned mind, referred to in Buddhism as the "turning about in the deepest seat of consciousness" (Govinda, 1969; Suzuki, 1987). However, in recognition of the difficulty of emancipating oneself from the compelling illusion of separateness, gurus serve as external guides and catalysts in both Buddhism and Hinduism for awakening a person to his or her true nature.

Not all teachers or religious institutions successfully resist the temptation to exploit their followers' dependency on them. By the Middle Ages, the Catholic Church had taken to dispensing grace through the sale of indulgences, which undermined its moral authority. In contemporary times, Jung was particularly articulate in underscoring the alienation that the Reformation fostered by disavowing the living symbols and sacerdotal functions that had once served to mediate God's felt presence in this world. "Protestantism," says Jung, "having divested itself from much of the ritual and codes of the Catholic Church, leaves the individual to confront his sins alone" (Jung, 1969, p. 34).

Implications for Modern Therapy

Systems-oriented family therapists have become adept at diagnosing dysfunctional triangles in relational therapy, and psychodynamic therapists have been trained to recognize and treat transference in the therapeutic setting. However, the concept of progressive triangulation in the spiritual journey may call for a broader view of triangulation and transference for the purposes of conducting therapy with individuals who are also seeking a closer relationship with higher power.

Given the function of mediators in spiritual traditions both East and West, it may be important for modern therapists to consider how they may be called upon to participate in progressive triangles that arise as a natural outgrowth of a client's spiritual aspirations.

Some therapists may reject outright playing a mentoring role in their clients' spiritual lives, much less becoming a symbol of a client's own higher power. That decision, of course, depends on a therapist's theoretical rational for practice. But as Jung was fond of saying, "Called or not called, God is present." Whether one interprets this statement from a metaphysical or a psychological standpoint, it is certainly true that the presence or absence of a felt sense of higher power comprises a significant aspect of psychotherapy, whether it is acknowledged or not. Consequently, a therapist's refusal to play an active role in the client's spiritual journey may merely keep the clients from exploring a crucially important part of their lives, and by implication, a valuable resource in their therapeutic process. In contrast, therapists who accept the role of mediator/mentor may perform a sacred function that is needed in this world without representing themselves as agents of any particular religious tradition, or as substitutes for priests and ministers.

In some cases, it is certainly wise to disqualify oneself from the mentoring/mediating role. For instance, a woman who, with her husband, had been seeing me for marital problems, asked me to become her spiritual mentor within the counseling relationship. I might have consented if I had been seeing her on an individual basis. But her renunciate spirituality had kept her aloof from emotional and sexual intimacy in her marriage, much to her husband's distress, and so I respectfully declined. My acquiescence would have created a non-therapeutic triangle weighted toward the wife's presumed interests, which would have surely alienated her husband.

In regard to those psychotherapeutic clients for whom I accept the additional role of spiritual mentor, I consider it important to discuss with them how spiritual mentoring relationships have a long history in Eastern and Western spiritual traditions, and that if the spiritual dimension of the relationship progresses as it should, the mentee will eventually experience a more direct connection with higher power. By keeping the client oriented to this goal, the therapist-mentor can minimize the chances that the client will become unduly attached to the mediator, or that either party will succumb to the "burdensome illusion" (Kopp, 1971; p. 96-97) that they are not spiritually equal.

Fortunately, there is a well-developed and emerging tradition of spiritual mentoring in Christianity, especially in the Catholic (Barry & Connolly, 1986) and Episcopalian churches (Edwards, 1980, 2001; Guenther, 1992; Hart, 1980; Jones, 1999; Leech, 2001). Further, recent works show an increasing ecumenical flavor (Anderson & Reese,1999; Bakke, 2000; Bumpus & Langer, 2005). Therapists who are inclined to augment their practice with spiritual mentoring will find that these authors exhibit a thorough awareness of the relationship between psychotherapy and spiritual mentoring and, without exception, advocate for their greater synthesis. Citing the current deficiencies in the traditional pathology-oriented field of mental health, Edwards says, ...lacking deep roots as a discipline in value theory, as well as in community (as opposed exclusively to intrapsychic) covenant, psychology is prone to certain blind spots that point to the needs for the complementary art of spiritual direction. (1980, p.)

Regardless of the authors' backgrounds, they agree on one thing in particular: The role of spiritual mentor confers no particular power or advantage. Instead, the mentor offers himself or herself as a spiritual friend or companion, who may differ from the mentee in terms of experience, but not in stature or power.

Summary and Discussion

Within the context of the psychotherapeutic relationship, progressive triangulation provides a way to understand a client's constructive impulse to search for a closer relationship with higher power through the mediating agency of the therapist. By embracing the teleological nature of this impulse, and abiding by the requirements of a progressive triangle, therapists can participate in a forward-looking emergence of the client's deeper relationship with higher power, which may in turn accelerate the therapeutic process. A psychotherapist who participates in a progressive triangle may effectively harness the impulse of the client's spiritual yearning as a way to recast the therapeutic endeavor, from an exclusive healing of past and current wounds and conflicts, to a process that is overshadowed by–and to some extent governed by—the client's spiritual unfoldment.

Triangles in the **spiritual life** resemble ordinary relationship triangles except, perhaps, in one significant regard: While ordinary dysfunctional triangles can ultimately be resolved by having the distanced parties communicate and accept responsibility for their respective contributions to the disengagement, triangles in the spiritual life cannot be resolved as long as the transcendent "other" remains remote from the seeker's experience. Because the experience of the transcendent tends to be elusive regardless of one's spiritual tradition, mediators may continue to play an important role throughout a seeker's life. Indeed, history reveals that the alternating focus between a direct and mediated relationship with the divine represents a timeless dialectic that cannot be resolved merely by rejecting one and asserting the importance of the other.

References

American Psychological Association. (1992). Ethical principles of psychologists and code of conduct.

American Psychiatric Association (2000). Diagnostic and Statistical Manual of Mental Disorders DSM-IV-TR. Arlington, VA: American Psychiatric Publishing

American Psychologist, 47, 1591–1611.

American Psychological Association (2002). Ethical principles of psychologists and code of conduct.

American Psychologist, 57, 1060–1073.

American Psychological Association. (2003). Guidelines on multicultural education, training, research, practice, and organizational change for psychologists. American Psychologist, 58, 377– 402.

American Psychological Association. (2006). Graduate study in psychology.Washington, DC: Author.

Anderson, K., Reese, R. (1999). Spiritual Mentoring: A Guide for Seeking and Giving Direction. Downers Grover, IL: Intervarsity Press

Bakke, J. A. (2000) Holy invitations: Exploring spiritual direction. Grand Rapids: Baker.

Barry, W. A, Connolly, W. J. (1986). The practice of spiritual direction. San Francisco: HarperSanFrancisco.

Blah, L. & Kohler, K. (2007). Shekinah. Retrieved November 29, 2007 from http://www.jewishencyclopedia.com/view.jsp?artid=588&letter=S#1940.

Bowen, M. (1978) Family therapy in clinical practice. New York: Jason Aronson.

Bradshaw, R. (1992). Montanism: Heresy or healthy revival? Retrieved November 22, 2007 from ttp://www.earlychurch.org.uk/article_montanism.html.

Bumpus, M. R., Langer, R. B. (2005) Supervision of spiritual directors: Engaging in holy mystery. New York: Morehouse.

Chadwick, H. (1986). The early Church. New York: Dorset.

Chidvalasananda, Gurumayi. Kindle my heart. South Fallsburg, NY: Syda Foundation.

Coleman, D. (1996). Positive sibling transference: Theoretical and clinical dimensions. Clinical Social Work Journal 24(4).

Collins, G. R. (1977). The rebuilding of psychology: An integration of psychology and Christianity. Wheaton, IL: Tyndale House.

Ellis, A. (1971). The case against religion: A psychotherapist's view. New York: Institute for Rational Living.

Edwards, T. H. (1980) Spiritual Friend: Reclaiming the gift of spiritual direction.

Edwards, T. H. (2001). Spiritual director, spiritual companion: Guide to tending the soul.

Ehrman, B. (2005). Lost Christianities: The battles for scripture and the faiths we never knew. Oxford: Oxford University Press.

Evans-wentz, W. Y., Gtsan-smyon He-ru-ka, Lopez, D. S. Jr., Zla-ba-bsam-'grub. (2000). Tibet's great yogi Milarepa : A biography from the Tibetan being the Jetsun-Kabbum or biographical history of Jetsun-Milarepa, according to the late Lama Kazi Dawa-Samdup's English rendering. New York: Oxford Univ. Press.

Feltham, C. (1999). Contextualising the therapeutic relationship. In C. Feltham (Ed.), Understanding the counselling relationship. London: Sage.

Fogarty, T. F. (1976). Systems concepts and dimensions of self. In Family therapy: Theory and practice, P. J. Guerin, ed., New York: Gardner

Freud, S. (1961). The future of an illusion (J. Strachey, Ed. and Trans.). New York: Norton. (Original work published 1927)

Gallup, G. (2006). The Gallup Poll: Public opinion 2006. Wilmington, DE: Scholarly Resources.

Hartz, G.W. (2005). Spirituality and mental health: Clinical applications. Binghamton, NY: Haworth Pastoral Press.

Hill, P., & Pargament, K. I. (2003). Advances in the conceptualization and measurement of religion and spirituality: Implications for physical and mental health research. American Psychologist, 58, 64–74.

Hart, T.n. The art of christian listening. Mahwah, NJ: Paulist

Leech, K. Soul friend. New York: Morehouse.

Mijolla, A. (ed) (2005). International Dictionary of Psychoanalysis. New York: Thomson/Gale.

Hoffman, L. (1981). Foundations of family therapy: A conceptual framework for systems change. New York: Basic Books.

Homans, P. (1995). Jung in context: Modernity and the making of a psychology. Chicago: University of Chicago Press.

James, W. (1890). Principles of psychology. New York: Holt.

James,W. (1902). The varieties of religious experience. Cambridge, MA: Harvard University Press.

Jung, C. G. (1938). Psychology and religion. New Haven, CT: Yale University Press.

Koenig, H. G. (1997). Is religion good for your health? The effects of religion on physical and mental health. Binghamton, NY: Haworth Pastoral Press.

Koenig, H. G., McCullough, M. E., & Larson, D. B. (2001). Handbook of religion and health. New York: Oxford University Press.

Lopez, S. J., & Snyder, C. R. (Eds.). (2003). Positive psychological assessment: A handbook of models and measures. Washington, DC: American Psychological Association.

McMinn, M. R., & Dominquez, A. W. (2005). Psychology and the church. Hauppauge, NY: Nova Science.

Miller, W. R. (Ed.). (1999). Integrating spirituality into treatment. Washington, DC: American Psychological Association.

Miller, W. R., & Thoresen, C. E. (2003). Spirituality, religion and health: An emerging research field. American Psychologist, 58, 24–35.

Myers, D. (2000). The American paradox: Spiritual hunger in a land of plenty. New Haven, CT: Yale University Press.

O'Hanlon, B. (2006). Pathways to spirituality: Connection, wholeness, and possibility for therapist and client. New York: Norton.

Pargament, K. I. (1997). The psychology of religious coping: Theory, research, practice. NewYork: Guilford Press.

Plante, T. G. (1999). A collaborative relationship between professional psychology and the Roman Catholic Church: A case example and suggested principles for success. Professional Psychology: Research and Practice, 30, 541–546.

Plante, T. G. (2004). Do the right thing: Living ethically in an unethical world. Oakland, CA: New Harbinger.

Plante, T. G., & Sharma, N. (2001). Religious faith and mental health outcomes. In T. G. Plante & A. C. Sherman (Eds.), Faith and health: Psychological perspectives (pp. 240–261). New York: Guilford Press.

Plante, T. G., & Sherman, A. S. (Eds.). (2001). Faith and health: Psychological perspectives. New York: Guilford Press.

Richards, P. S., & Bergin, A. E. (1997). A spiritual strategy for counseling and psychotherapy. Washington, DC: American Psychological Association.

Russell, S. R., & Yarhouse, M. A. (2006). Religion/spirituality within APA-accredited psychology predoctoral internships. Professional Psychology: Research and Practice, 37, 430– 436.

Shafranske, E. P. (2001). The religious dimensions of patient care within rehabilitation medicine: The role of religious attitudes, beliefs, and professional practices. In T. G. Plante & A. C. Sherman (Eds.), Faith and health: Psychological perspectives (pp. 311–338). New York: Guilford Press.

Sloan, R. P., Bagiella, E., & Powell, T. (1999). Religion, spirituality, and medicine. The Lancet, 353, 664– 667.

Sloan, R. P., Bagiella, E., & Powell, T. (2001).Without a prayer: Methodological problems, ethical challenges, and misrepresentations in the study of religion, spirituality, and medicine. In T. G.

Plante & A. C. Sherman (Eds.), Faith and health: Psychological perspectives (pp. 339–354). New York: Guilford Press.

Sperry, L., & Shafranske, E. P. (Eds.). (2005). Spiritually oriented psychotherapy.Washington, DC: American Psychological Association.

Watson, J. B. (1983). Psychology from the standpoint of a behaviorist. Dover, NH: Pinter. (Original work published 1924)

List of Contributors

1. **Prof. R. P. Sharma**, Ex. Head and Dean, Dept. of Education, University of Delhi, Delhi

2. **Dr. Neelam Mehta Bali**, Associate Professor, M.V. College of Education (Delhi University)

3. **Arbind Kumar Jha**, Associate Professor, Central University of Himachal Pradesh, Ph.D., RBS College of Education, Rewari-123401, Haryana, (INDIA); Emails: *drarbind1@gmail.com*

4. **Dr. Reena Kannojiya**, Assistant Professor, Department of Philosophy, Miranda House, University of Delhi, Delhi-110007, India; E-mail. reena kannojiya@ayahoo.com; Mobile: 9811445013

5. **Ms. Savita Sharma**, Advocate, Supreme Court, Delhi

6. **Dr. Naraginti Amareswaran**, Researcher, Dept. of Education, Sri Venkateswara University, Tirupati-517502, Andhra Pradesh, E-mail: *amareswaran@gmail.com*, Mobile: 09441910359

7. **Dr. S.K. Panneer Selvam**, Assistant Professor, Dept. of Education, Bharathidasan University, Tiruchurapalli, Tamil Nadu, E-mail: *skpskpbdu@gmail.com*, Mobile: 09443071987

8. **Dr. Arti Srivastava**, Army Institute of Education, Delhi Cantt.

9. **Dr. G.K. Joneja**, Associate Professor, NCERT, New Delhi

10. **Pranita Gopal**, Asst Professor, Army Institute of Education, Delhi Cantt. New Delhi 110010, Email: pranitagopal@gmail.com

11. **Dr. Aradhana Mani**, Amity Institute of Education, Amity Universit, Noida, India, Email: aradhanamani@yahoo.co.in arnavmani@gmail.com

12. **Dr. Manisha Minocha**, Principal, KIRAS, New Delhi

    Dr. Monica Auplish, Assistant Professor, KIRAS, New Delhi

13. **Swami Atmapriyananda**, Vice Chancellor, Ramakrishna Mission Vivekananda University (Declared by Govt. of India as a Deemed University under Section 3 of UGC Act, 1956) PO Belur Math, Dist Howrah, West Bengal

14. **Dr. Sadhana Srivastava**, Ph.D. Botany, Computer Professional, New Greenfield School, New Delhi

15. **Dr. Neerja Dhankar**, Principal, Army Institute of Education

16. **Prof. Gouri Srivastava**, Head, Department of Women's Studies, NCERT

17. **Dr. Y.P. Anand**, Former Chairman, Railway Board, & Director, National Gandhi Museum, New Delhi, 513, Pocket C, Sector A, Vasantkunj, New Delhi-110070; Ph. 26898913, 9312700812

18. **Amita Puri**, Army Inst. of Education, Delhi Cantt.